LIVING MEDITATION

A journey beyond body and mind

LIVING MEDITATION

A journey beyond body and mind

HECTOR ESPONDA DUBIN

RADHA SOAMI SATSANG BEAS

Published by:
Sewa Singh, Secretary
Radha Soami Satsang Beas
Dera Baba Jaimal Singh
Punjab 143 204, India

First edition   2004

11 10 09 08 07 06 05 04   8 7 6 5 4 3 2 1

ISBN: 81-8256-050-0

Printed in India by: Baba Barkha Nath Printers, New Delhi 110 015

Whether the answer to your question is in six pages or in a book or in one line, the answer is the same: meditation! It depends upon how much time you want to take to understand that answer—whether by reading the whole book or by understanding only one or two words.

Maharaj Charan Singh

Contents

Introduction

As long as you do not die while living
How will you obtain true benefit?
Therefore, die and come out of your body.
You have died many times,
Yet still you remain behind the veil
For the method of true dying
You did not learn.

Rumi

There is a method to conquer death. From Masters of spirituality we understand that there is a way to experience the life that exists beyond the death of the body, and a method or technique we can learn to experience it. These spiritual Masters teach the way to leave our body at will and return to it when we decide to do so. From them we learn that by practising the method, by applying it to our daily lives, we can embark on a journey beyond body and mind, and in the process, develop clear thinking, peace of mind and inner joy. The Masters tell us that by perfecting their method we gain liberation from the cycle of death and birth and experience eternal bliss.

The spiritual Masters teach us that in the body the soul is knotted together with the mind at the spiritual eye centre located in our forehead. From this point, our attention spreads out into the material creation where it constantly absorbs worldly impressions. The continuous, outward-directed activity of the mind, fuelled most often by our desires, forms deep impressions in our consciousness. These impressions act like complex, many-layered blankets, concealing from us the brilliance, power and vitality of our life force, our soul.

When the light of the soul becomes obscured by the mind, we begin to perceive the things of the world as if they were permanent and capable of giving us true happiness. Deceived by a distorted view of reality, we fail to realize that the events, people and things in our lives bring us a happiness that, by its very nature, is only superficial and short-lived. We fail to see that chasing happiness through whatever we are attached to in the perishable world has to lead, sooner or later, to frustration and sorrow while at the same time increasing our karmic debt. Tempted and driven by our senses, we keep doing things that sow the seeds for future incarnations in the physical plane. Mistakenly, we direct our attention to the objects of our affection because we believe the reason for our joy or pain lies in them. In this way, our distorted view of reality leads to actions that drive the roots of our consciousness ever deeper into lower planes of existence. This strengthens the downward tendencies of our mind and keeps us from seeing the light of our soul. The sad result of this downward spiral—a spiral of cause and effect—is that the soul becomes so trapped and hidden in the lower physical realms that the time soon comes when the soul's very existence is no longer even acknowledged.

I know those habits that can ruin your life
Still send their invitations ...

Learn to recognize the counterfeit coins
That may buy you just a moment of pleasure,
But then drag you for days
Like a broken man
Behind a farting camel.

Hafiz

The way to break free from the limitations we have imposed on ourselves, to regain the clarity that reflects our highest potential, is to empower our soul consciousness through meditation. Once we begin to practise meditation, we soon realize that the method of the Masters is a path, journey or way for us to live. It is the path of becoming masters of our mind and senses. To follow the path to its destination means nothing less than the journey of a lifetime. As we travel along it and our mind becomes steadier through the practice of meditation, we will experience the soul gaining control while the undisciplined and ever-troublesome aspects of our mind are progressively weakened. Life becomes more carefree, we are controlled less by our desires, and we find ourselves more balanced and content. As the soul gains the upper hand, the benefits of meditation are increasingly felt and our spiritual resolve becomes deeper and firmer. We are no longer as easily deceived by a distorted perspective, and when we face hard times it is easier to deal with them and recover our balance.

Constantly mastering his mind,
The spiritual man grows peaceful,
Attains supreme bliss,
And returns to the Absolute One.

Bhagavad Gita

Many Masters of spirituality throughout the ages stand witness, through their lives and writings, to the success of the method of Shabd meditation, and this book is about its practice.

Shabd, a Sanskrit name for the divine power, is known in different cultures by many different names: Tao, Holy Ghost, Word, Cosmic Energy, Buddha Nature, Kalma, Holy Sound, Sound Current, Truth and many others. The names themselves are not important. What matters is where they point. Shabd, as we use the term in this book, is the eternal reality underlying all forms of life. Shabd is beyond but also within every life form. This means that it is within everyone, within every form of life. It is accessible to each one of us as our deepest Self. Some might think of this reality as God, but while neither 'Shabd' nor 'God' can do justice to the transcendental reality they refer to, in this book the word 'Shabd' has been preferred to the word 'God'.

The word God carries for most people the connotation of someone or something outside of oneself, whereas the word Shabd as power or energy—a word that is unfamiliar to many people—allows for an open concept that does not connote a being out there, apart from and outside of what and who we are. The word Shabd, as used in this book, includes inner as well as outer eternal reality. The concept does not reduce the limitless to a limited finite entity. Shabd is every thing. It is in every body. It is our own essence. It is our reality.

> The beginning and end of all things is Shabd. All gross matter, the sky and so forth, subtle matter, sound, form, taste and scent are all Shabd. Whatever exists is Shabd. Whatever is manifested from Shabd cannot be anything but Shabd. Shabd is our creator. Shabd is our sustainer. We are of Shabd and Shabd is ours.
>
> Maharaj Sawan Singh

By practising Shabd meditation we learn how to contact and merge with Shabd, the divine and primal power, in full consciousness. We learn how to 'die' to our limited self so that we can become alive forever. Freed from identification with our body selves, we gain freedom from personal obsessions, suffering and attachments. We learn how to access the positive creative energy or power that is already within us. The method of Shabd meditation comes recommended to us by Masters of spirituality, called here Shabd Masters, who have lived by its principles and experienced the truth of the practice. That, for us, is its guarantee. To know that what they say is true, we must put their method into practice and experience it for ourselves. Only through action can we know that it is true. Only through action will we experience how the integral system of the Shabd Masters can help us become complete human beings, attain knowledge of the deathless Self and realize the divine. The Shabd Masters assure us that if we apply their method in full, we will move from a world of concepts to one of spiritual experience. Through practice, we will be personally transformed.

There is a difference between knowing the path and walking it.

Morpheus to Neo in *The Matrix*

True Masters of spirituality always impart their method and teachings free of charge. Their method rests on a foundation of four fundamental principles: following a vegetarian diet, not taking alcohol or mind-altering substances, living a moral and honest life, and giving at least one tenth of one's time daily to the practice of meditation. The first three principles support the fourth, which is the key to self-transformation. It is an interdependent and interlinking system: all four principles have to be put into practice rigorously, for otherwise, the integral system cannot work.

A vegetarian diet is necessary to minimize the consequences resulting from the violence and cruelty of killing for food. Unless the burden we bear as the consequence of doing such actions (our karmas) is kept to the minimum, we cannot hope to rise spiritually. Concentration is the key to gaining conscious access to Shabd. Since blowing the mind with drugs or dulling it with alcohol sabotages all serious concentration, it is essential to abstain from drugs and alcohol. It is also important that we lead a moral and honest life, for unless we are able to control our emotions at the level of physical actions, how can we hope to direct them constructively at the more subtle level within ourselves? If we give free rein to our passions and desires, we will soon find ourselves driven by them. Our attention will remain trapped in lower, physical centres, and it will be impossible to raise it to the level where concentration begins. If meditation is the means whereby we transform our consciousness, then giving just one tenth of our daily time to its practice is the least we must do. How can we succeed in a profession if we don't give time to it? How can we enjoy a destination if we don't make the time needed to travel there?

Through these four principles, the Masters set clear guidelines for a way of life that supports our spiritual goal. The guidelines serve as painted lines on a road. The moment we cross a line, we know we have deviated from our course and are in danger. The Masters, however, impress upon us the importance of using our personal sense of discrimination. Within the four broad parameters, it is up to each one of us to find out which actions or thoughts will strengthen or weaken our spiritual life, which actions and thoughts will take us towards our destination and which will take us further away.

Other tools that help us support our meditation practice are listening to spiritual discourses (*satsang*), reading spiritual literature, and service (*seva*) to the Master. Seva can be done through service to our spiritual community (*sangat*) or to our community in general. The advantage of serving our spiritual community is that it puts us under the direct orders of our Master. Such service develops the relationship of disciple and Master—a discipline that is key to the transformative process of the spiritual path.

We can further support our spiritual objective by being selective about the things we choose to see, hear, talk or think about, and the company we keep. In addition, it is easier to practise meditation with a fit and healthy body, so it is desirable to care for our body by taking steps to promote its health and well-being. All these practices will support our efforts to bring our attention to the spiritual eye centre and begin the journey to reach our source.

The ways of reaching our source are many, but all the paths at some point merge into the universal path of travelling within oneself through Shabd, through spiritual Light and Sound. Most of us are at the very early stages of the journey. Few have had actual experience of the truth that is our goal. This book, therefore, has been prepared to inspire us to move from concepts to experience. Since we aspire to reach that point where we actually experience the Shabd, this book highlights the irreplaceable importance, value and practical impact of meditation, and how, without meditation, we will reach nowhere.

The book looks at our personal responsibilities as disciples on the spiritual path and explains how a clear understanding of the teachings can lead us to the daily practice of meditation, without shirking our responsibilities. Clear thinking, a positive attitude and sincere effort support spiritual priorities and help us focus on daily meditation. Through the practice of meditation we become clear, we become positive and we gain mastery over our mind. Ultimately, through the practice of meditation, we obtain the supreme peace and joy that result from being spiritually transformed and freed of all limitations.

To emphasize the universality of the path of Shabd meditation, the book includes quotations not only from Sant Mat (the path of the Shabd Masters), but also from different traditions, times and places. The simple method of Shabd meditation, the method of dying to the world and awakening to the divine, arises naturally from fundamentals of human nature common to all humanity. It is a universal method or mystic way, common to all true Masters of spirituality, whatever their language, religion, culture or the context in which they taught.

> All rivers merge in the Ocean.
> The Ocean refuses no river.
> > Indian proverb

1

Spiritual beings
going through a human experience

This life is but a link in an infinite chain of existence.
The body perishes but the soul lives on—immortal,
treading the path back from its painful separation to
its blissful return to the mansions of the Lord.
                                          Maharaj Jagat Singh

Mystics tell us that although we are in a body, we are not the body—we are spiritual beings going through the experience of being human. From this encouraging point of view, we are pure beings of spiritual nature already, but beings whose purity has been temporarily obscured by our mind and senses. We will realize this for ourselves only when our soul dominates our mind, and this higher state of consciousness, the Masters tell us, can be gained through meditation, and through meditation alone.

Through meditation, we learn to hold our attention still at the spiritual eye centre. Once we are able to do this, the mind comes under the influence of the soul and is receptive to the more subtle reality of the Shabd. The layers of ever-changing desires and worldly impressions that conceal our pure consciousness fall away naturally—the scales of spiritual blindness fall from our eyes—and we experience, with the ear and eye of the spirit, the sweetness and power of the deathless Self, the Shabd, buried deep within us. Without the practice of meditation, our mind remains possessed by worldly passions and attachments, and our soul, deprived of its best potential ally—an enlightened mind— travels without support through the experience of being human in this most dangerous of planes, the land of Kal.

The Indian word 'Kal' has been deliberately kept here, as there is no equivalent to this concept in the Western tradition. 'Kal' in Sanskrit literally means time—the illusion of life un- folding in sequence. In the teachings of the saints, Kal is per- sonified as the ruler of the realms of mind and matter, god of the material universe—the physical, astral and causal planes where time shapes and destroys all—whereas the Supreme Conscious- ness exists both within and beyond time.

According to the Shabd Masters, it is Kal that keeps the soul trapped in the material and mental spheres, where mind and matter, not spirit, dominate. The way out of this trap is to transcend the realm of mind and matter by means of Shabd meditation under the guidance of a living Shabd Master—a guide who is free from the prisons of time and duality, and whose perspective reflects to his or her disciples the unlimited truth of Shabd.

> In his Radiant Form, he [the Master] helps the disciple
> at every step, accompanying him throughout the spiritual
> journey.
>
> Maharaj Charan Singh

Life in the land of Kal

> Look upon the world as a bubble: him who looks thus upon
> the world the king of death does not see. Come, look at this
> world, resembling a painted royal chariot. The foolish are
> sunk in it; for the wise, there is no attachment for it.
>
> The Dhammapada

When we stay at a hotel, we don't try to fix the problems we face.
This is because we are guests at the hotel, not attached to it, and
we know we will soon be on our way. Similarly, a bridge is meant
for crossing, so no one builds his home, the place where he is to
stay, on a bridge. Is it not strange, then, that even though we know
we will not be in the world permanently, we act as if we were to be
here forever! Soami Ji says that we are so attached to the creation
and love it so much that we have forgotten the Lord, forgotten
our true home, and forgotten who we really are. We are trapped
in this world of illusion and take everything that we see to be real.

Not only mystics tell us that this is a world of illusion, scientists say the same thing. Science tells us that at the subatomic or
quantum level, nothing of the material world is left intact. There
are only energy fields with no solidity at all, nothing for the senses
to see or touch. Our physical senses are too dull and too slow to
sense, feel, see or experience in any manner these energy fields
that are in fact vibrations taking place in a void. All the suns,
stars and galaxies in the whole cosmos are a quantum mirage,
winking in and out of existence millions of times per second. The
whole universe is like a blinking light. The illusion in which we
exist isn't restricted to the material world. Our mental perceptions,
emotions and attachments are part of the illusory realm of mind
and matter.

Meditation is the means to realize the fleeting and imperma-
nent nature of human life, of all our attachments and endeavours—
even life itself. Meditation is the means to realize a higher, more
permanent level of reality. Through meditation and with the help
of a true Master, we can wake up from the dream-like existence
that characterizes lower planes of consciousness. The Masters
teach that just as it is the very nature of the world to change un-
ceasingly, so it is the privilege of human beings to experience the
changeless, deathless and blissful nature of their own true Self.

Yet how difficult it is to retain the spiritual perspective and
clarity as we live out our daily lives in the material world! Wherever we look, we see change, suffering and conflict. Influenced
by what is going on around us, we easily take the path of least
resistance. How natural it can seem to go with the flow—so we
too 'flow' with the downward, superficial tendencies that appear
to characterize our times, even though our Master demonstrates
the benefits of choosing the upward path and shows us how to
disengage ourselves from all and everything that pulls us down.

> Everyone is burning in the fire of maya [illusion]; all are
> roasting in it day and night.
>
> Baba Jaimal Singh

Injustice, sickness and poverty are everywhere, and we see
cheating, violence and obsession with sense gratification all
around, but for us to capitulate to a negative perspective of life is
to deny our spiritual nature and invite restlessness and suffering
upon ourselves. To go to the extent of indulging in the downward tendencies of the mind is simply asking for yet another birth
and inviting even more suffering upon ourselves.

In a place where mind and matter are active, there can never be peace. Sorrows and wars of nations, or communities, or individuals shall continue. The soul must seek other planes to find peace. To find peace is the business of the individual. Everybody has to seek it within himself.

Maharaj Sawan Singh

To choose a positive path is to affirm one's spiritual nature. All conflict, in the final analysis, is the manifestation of inner conflict. And while we may never be able to make the world into a utopia, we can, the saints tell us, transform ourselves. Through the practice of meditation, we can gradually reclaim for ourselves a higher state of being. By turning inwards, by exploring and experiencing the spiritual reality of inner life, we can gain the strength of character to remain sane even if the entire world were to go crazy around us. Problems in life will always be present— it is the nature of the realm of Kal—but the support we get from meditation will make us increasingly able to deal with the ups and downs of daily life.

> Pleasures from external objects
> Are wombs of suffering.
> They have their beginnings and their ends;
> No wise man seeks joy among them.
>
> *Bhagavad Gita*

We are responsible for the freedom of our soul

> Liberty means responsibility.
> That is why most men dread it.
>
> George Bernard Shaw

To acknowledge and affirm our spiritual nature, the first practical step we are to take once we are committed to the spiritual path is to embrace responsibility for our every thought and action. If it is Kal's responsibility to keep us trapped in the realms of suffering, it is equally the responsibility of each human being to take the future of his or her soul in hand.

Whatever we are today, it is the result of what we thought and did in the past. By the same rule of cause and effect, what we are to become in the future will be determined by what we think and do right now, today. Through our consciousness, our sense of discrimination, we can choose at every moment to make a difference now, in this life, not only for the rest of our lifetime but for all eternity. This is our privilege. This is our challenge.

While the body we occupy at this point in time will die, our soul continues far beyond this life to reap the harvest of the choices we are making here and now. If we are clever and make wise choices today about what we think and do, it will be a lot easier to make positive choices tomorrow. That we have been put on the path of the Masters means the time has now come, in this very life, to become masters of ourselves. There will be no incarnation better than the one we are in now. It is now that we have the opportunity to realize who and what we are.

Why, then, would we wait for another birth? Why do we wait to make meditation our first priority? If we are not going to make this effort now, when are we going to do it? We need to ask ourselves these questions. If it is not for me to do it, who do I think will do this work for me? Why, we can ask ourselves, did we come to this path? Why, then, do we procrastinate? We made a conscious choice to accept the teachings of a Shabd Master for good reason. To help us keep our focus, we need constantly to revisit our motives and our priorities.

Now is the time to get serious about living the teachings! There is no better time to make the required effort to keep our attention in the eye centre. The responsibility is ours and ours alone. No one else can do it for us. If a student wants to pass an exam, he or she has to study; no one else can do the studying for them. Master Sawan Singh (also known as Great Master) says: "Develop the power to withdraw your attention, *at will*, from the outward objects and from the physical body, and concentrate it in the eye focus."

He states the disciple's responsibility very clearly. Those words 'at will' mean it is we who are responsible for keeping our mind in the eye centre through effort and self-control. No one else will do it for us. Even the Master, who is teaching, guiding and protecting us, will not do it for us. Unless we take this step ourselves, we will never make spiritual progress.

With the gift of initiation, Master bestows on the disciple sufficient grace to do meditation. All disciples of a true Master have the strength to meditate and to keep the attention at the eye focus. We cannot let laziness or fear paralyze us. We have the strength to raise our attention to the eye centre because the force that is upholding the entire creation is upholding us. That force is Shabd; that is what the Master is; and that, too, is what we are.

The power within is not ignorant of what you are doing. It is with you and constantly watches you and guides you.

Maharaj Sawan Singh

Initiation is not an insurance policy

One does not become a satsangi simply by being initiated.

Maharaj Jagat Singh

Sant Mat is not an insurance policy by which we are guaranteed salvation just by attending initiation. Although initiation is no small matter, although it marks the culmination of a journey of thousands of lifetimes, it is not the end of the journey. Shabd Master Baba Gurinder Singh (or Baba Ji, as he is known) tells us that the event of our initiation may be taken as the projection of our desire to grow spiritually. Unless we take action, we will not become satsangis. A satsangi is one who is in contact with Truth (*sat*, truth; *sang*, with). You are either there, or you are not there. There is no half-way ground in experiencing Truth.

As Master Jagat Singh (or Sardar Bahadur, as he was also known) points out, we do not become satsangis by the mere act of having attended initiation. A graduate student enrolling in a doctoral programme does not become a PhD just by joining the university. A student has to attend classes for many years before he or she graduates. Until we have merged into Shabd, we are all seekers in search of our home. The way to go home is through meditation. If we are not doing our meditation, then we are not on our way to becoming satsangis. Nor are we following the teachings of the Master, no matter how often we have the sight or company *(darshan)* of his physical form, listen to satsangs, do seva or read spiritual books. Without meditation, it is impossible to attain liberation.

A Master comes to initiate us, to put us in contact with our inner Master, the Shabd. Once we have been initiated, we have to follow the instructions our living Master has given us. By putting more emphasis on the person of the Master than on his teachings, we make a serious mistake that is detrimental to our spiritual welfare. The Master's finger is pointing to the eye centre but we are busy worshipping his finger, not looking at where his finger is pointing. If we believe that Master will wave a magic wand and automatically give us liberation after death, we are wrong. If we believe that just by attending initiation or by having his physical darshan, without doing our meditation, he will give us liberation after death, we are also sadly mistaken.

Shabd Master Charan Singh used to say that nothing justifies us saying that we cannot do meditation. The Master fulfils his task by immersing us in an ocean of grace. Now we have to do our part and take responsibility, through action, for the welfare of our soul.

Kal's deadliest weapon: indulging in thinking

> Mind is the deadliest of foes, but the most useful of servants. When it turns wild and gets out of control, it heads for certain destruction. When properly awakened and controlled, there is no limit to what the mind can do.
>
> Maharaj Charan Singh

Once we have been initiated, we need to practise the process of controlling our mind so that it becomes the servant and ally of our soul, not our master. As we all have experienced, there is no end to our desires, and we know how easy it is to be dominated by them! At the root of this problem lies the habit of giving free rein to our mind so that it goes wherever the senses lead it. If we learn to control our mind, we automatically gain control over our

senses. In *Die to Live*, Master Charan Singh says: "Intellect is
a great barrier in our way, but we have to pierce the barrier of
intellect with the help of intellect."

Used constructively, the intellect is a great friend on the spiritual journey. Supported by a spiritual focus and the habit of clear
thinking, the mind discriminates for our spiritual advantage—
looking to our spiritual growth and spiritual well-being. 'Compulsive' thinking, on the other hand, fuels desires, makes the ego
stronger and contradicts all efforts to put our soul in charge.
Compulsive, out-of-control thinking gets us into trouble and
leads to pain. It is a question of who is in control. Allowed to go
its own way, not referring to its power of discrimination, the mind
quickly becomes our downfall.

'Compulsive' thinking is the process of abandoning oneself
to the inner chatter of the mind. It is the tendency to live in a
world of concepts and illusions; of fear for what the future may
bring; of obsessing with planning; of remembering and ruminat-
ing on what is past. The process itself builds habits of worrying,
judging, analyzing, building expectations and daydreaming.
Compulsive thinking feeds the passions. It reinforces the ego.
Constant mental repetition of the obsessions of the day makes
deep grooves in the mind. These grooves become so deep that
even if we act on them, we may not be able even in one lifetime
to wipe clean the slate of karmas. Then we have to reincarnate
again—in response to what remains on the slate.

Relentlessly and restlessly, the mind tries to experience and
enjoy everything. But nothing seems to satisfy its ravenous
hunger. The acquisition of wealth and power gives rise to
endless desires. Our possessions become the master, instead of being our slave. The passions gradually forge

heavy chains around us, bind us to the baser things of the
world and invariably harden our heart.

Maharaj Charan Singh

We generate thousands of thoughts every day. From the spiritual perspective this means that thousands of times a day our
mind bypasses the eye centre as we run from one thought to the
next without rest or pause. No wonder we feel restless and anxious! How could it be otherwise, with all that activity going on
within our head? When we indulge in wanton thinking, we waste
many opportunities to centre ourselves through spiritual repetition (simran). We miss the benefit that is available to us—the
well-being that comes from repeating the words the Master gave
us at the time of initiation, through which we create that much-
needed focus at the eye centre.

If, rather than containing the mind's activity, we continuously
indulge its whims and allow it to do as it pleases, then it continues
to jump around wildly, wanting to go its own way. And it does
this even more at the one time we really need it to become still,
when we try to pin it down during the meditation period.

Masters therefore encourage less indulging in thinking and
more focused repetition. Indulging the mind has an adverse effect
on the disciple, scattering the attention and preventing us from
going within. Since karma originates from action, and action
originates from thought, by constantly thinking about small,
insignificant, passing desires we fan these desires into forest fires.
First, there is a thought or an idea—in the beginning it may seem
just an innocent thought wave, one that can be easily brushed
aside by a wave of simran or a counter-thought. However, if the
mind starts to dwell on the thought, it becomes a desire. Once
the desire gains momentum, it takes hold of us and we begin to

consider how we can 'possess' the desired object. A great thirst
and appetite may soon develop for it, and we become restless
until we satisfy our desire. Once action has taken place, we have
created karma. Craving, or mental indulgence, is thus the womb
of all the invisible chains and fetters that bind us to this world.

If, on the other hand, we choose simran to focus our mind
and brush away these extraneous thoughts when they are just
beginning, we pre-empt the battle. We cut at the root of our
desires, dilute the downward tendencies of the mind and win a
victory for our soul. One by one, each of these little victories adds
up and gradually the positive energy they generate helps us establish our attention at the eye centre from where the currents of
spiritual energy power our soul.

The habit of compulsive thinking is a form of mental diar-
rhoea that weakens us, a sickness that prevents us from fulfilling
our spiritual potential. It is a pathological state of human nature,
a misdirected use by the mind of the power or energy of the
soul. Not only does compulsive thinking weaken the spirit and
strengthen the ego, it inexorably reinforces the mistaken notions
that the world is permanent and that other people and events
are responsible for our problems.

> While the mind derives its life-force and energy from the
> soul, it at the same time does everything possible to suffocate
> the soul!
>
> Maharaj Sawan Singh

The way to treat this sickness is to concentrate and focus our
attention at the eye centre through simran. Simran reduces and
quietens the stressful static created by out-flowing thought waves.
Simran restores the mind to clarity, strength and wellness. Simran

frees us from our obsessions so that we can be empty of our petty self and become receptive to the healing power of the Shabd within. (For more on this subject, see the section on simran in Chapter 5.)

Get a grip on reality

> Satsangis should form the habit of 'thinking'—clear thinking … Clear thinking is ninety percent *abhyas* [spiritual practice]. Clear thinking is a blessing. It can easily be attained by a little practice.
>
> Maharaj Jagat Singh

As we walk the spiritual path, we come to understand more and more that our suffering is rooted in our distorted or unclear way of perceiving the world and ourselves. By perceiving reality in a delusional way, we construct a delusional reality within which we live. It is no wonder, then, that when we experience lust, greed or any of the downward tendencies, we define ourselves through them, through our thoughts and emotions. Deluded as we are, we identify our very being with our anger, lust, greed, attachments and our ego. As we go through the experience of being human, we confuse our real Self with what we feel.

The greatest tragedy of our deluded state is that we fail to see that our essence is Shabd. The Masters tell us that even the smallest part of Shabd is nothing but light, bliss and love. From the encouraging perspective of the Masters, our obsessions and neuroses are but temporary obstructions, passing dark clouds that block the brilliance of our soul from reaching us. Our challenge is to contribute to the process that drives the clouds away.

Meditation helps us reach a state where we can detach ourselves from our emotions and obsessions. Through Shabd meditation, we actually experience that we are not these ever-changing identities that we assume through our feelings and neuroses, but that we are fundamentally pure and constant. We are not the small self we thought we were, but rather the Shabd Self—this light, bliss and love that is within us. Through meditation we realize that our downward tendencies are superficial and temporary. As we stop identifying ourselves with our passions and attachments, we let go of them. Once we let go of them, we are free to identify with our Shabd Self. Meditation helps us to gain increasing clarity as to who we really are.

As the meditation practice becomes stabilized, we begin to see the process of life in an objective manner. We see events and people for what they are, rather than for what we have always projected on them. It becomes possible to witness that our thoughts and emotions are just that: thoughts and emotions, personal mental projections or electrical impulses. Seeing these projections in a clear light, we release our grip. The resulting light-heartedness we experience enables us to go deeper into the meditation practice. The deeper we go, the more clearly we understand the true nature of the mind.

Strengthened by meditation, we are able to watch how the mind, in expressing itself, creates infinite scenarios and then dissolves them again. We see for ourselves how its reservoir is unlimited, how there is no end to its creations. We start to recognize that the source of our problems lies in the deceptive nature of our mental creations, and in our yearning for permanent or lasting solutions in an ever-changing world. Because we treat the world as permanent, we look to it for the lasting happiness we crave. Clear thinking shows us that it is this, our distorted perception, that is leading us again and again to seek happiness in situations where the final outcome can only, by its nature, be frustration, separation and pain.

Clear thinking is attained by practice, and it is well worth cultivating it to help us avoid falling into our own mind traps. We can help ourselves by reasoning things out and thinking things through in the light of the saints' spiritual perspective; by using common sense to see if what we think seems reasonable, logical and truthful; by checking if our conclusions will bring us closer to or further from our spiritual goal. Real clarity, however, will be achieved only when the currents of thought settle, when through the practice of simran they become tranquil at our eye centre.

Clear thinking takes us deeper in the practice of meditation. Once the thought waves are stilled, our soul experiences a higher reality through its faculty of direct perception. With our shifting mind anchored, we perceive things and remain unaffected by them, so that we are able to let life go its own way. Thus a two-way process is created: as we think clearly, it becomes easier to concentrate in meditation; and increased concentration, leading to the unperturbed receptivity of a heightened consciousness, allows the Shabd to be revealed.

If the doors of perception were cleansed, everything would appear as it is, infinite.

William Blake

To be able to keep our attention in the eye centre, it is critical that at the time of meditation we let go of many things that may otherwise demand our attention. It is critical that we remind ourselves that it is our *perception* of events and other people that affects us; it is our *perception* of life that makes us suffer, rather than the people and things themselves. If we are able to realize this fact and let go of our obsessions, then it becomes easier for us to achieve better concentration in our meditation practice. The one strengthens the other. This is why it is crucial that we put full effort into exercising control over our thoughts.

With clear thinking, we see that many of the preoccupations that prevent us from doing simran are not worth pursuing. They are personal, based on our own misconceptions, and have no lasting relevance. For instance, our impulse to blame circumstances or people is a self-deception. We realize that events or people don't hurt us; it is how we view the world that makes us feel hurt. Events are impersonal; others are not to blame; it is our own perception that is at fault. What others think or say about us is not in our control: people's opinions are their own, so we shouldn't let our meditation be perturbed by them. People may not be what we wish them to be since each and every person has to go through his or her own personal and individual drama. Given the law of karma, therefore, it is foolish to think we can bend or shape other people to suit our own life's drama.

Open your eyes: see things for what they really are, thereby sparing yourself the pain of false attachments and avoidable devastation.

Epictetus

Events such as beginning or ending a relationship, power struggles at our place of work or seva, getting ill, becoming rich or poor—none of these is under our control. Most of these events were already determined and charted out before we were born by our own actions in previous births. We would derive far more benefit if we worked to control our thinking instead of trying to control events, people or circumstances. What would we gain if we were to control the whole world, but could not control ourselves!

The fact is that we don't have a choice regarding many things that happen to us, but we do have the choice as to how we react to them. Will we react in a positive manner? This choice can be ours. Will we turn our attention towards our inner life? If so, what will we choose there? We have the choice to choose simran or to occupy ourselves with inner chatter: will we let go of our apparent need to be entertained, ad nauseam, by our own thoughts and dreams? We have the choice to cultivate receptivity to the Sound. Will we give our time to our meditation practice? We have the choice to calm our mind, to cultivate clear thinking, to choose a path of inner happiness and inner freedom. Will we keep working with ourselves to strengthen our simran? What will we choose?

> Happiness and freedom begin with a clear understanding
> of one principle: some things are within our control, and
> some things are not.
>
> Epictetus

Invert the five passions to nurture meditation

Clear thinking helps us redirect the emotions and thoughts that hinder our meditation, yet it is interesting to note that when it comes to spirituality the mind is so perverse that it turns everything backwards. On the spiritual path, we talk about how we want to replace lust, anger, greed, attachment and pride or ego with their opposite virtues so as to nurture our meditation. Do we succeed? What seems to happen more often is that the mind comes in and twists everything around.

For example, lust is excessive indulgence in the senses while the opposite of lust is continence—but where do we, who see ourselves as spiritual practitioners, practise continence? Is it not frequently seen in the spiritual side of life, where many of us— ironically—practise continence in the area of meditation! We may even say that too much meditation is dangerous! How often, on the other hand, do we justify being lustful for life "for the experience of it"? "I need to have this experience." "I need to know this thing." "I need to go through this."

As disciples on a spiritual adventure it should be the opposite. On the spiritual path, we should be lustful for meditation. If we are passionate about spirituality, we have to crave and yearn after meditation. We need to nurture the desire for more indulgence in meditation until we reach the point that we lose ourselves in it.

Another passion we can redirect to improve our meditation is anger. When someone in this world does something we don't like, the most common response is to react and to try to change that person. We get angry because the world isn't the way we want it to be. "This person is no good." "I want you to be this way." We are filled with anger. But when we come to our meditation, it is nothing but forgiveness. Where is our reforming zeal when we are dealing with ourselves? Do we try to change our mind by giving it a good slap in the face and saying, "You are going to sit! You are going to meditate!" Oh no, we become all forgiveness. We say, "Oh, poor mind, it is too much for you. If I press you too hard, you will rebel and overwhelm me. I forgive you, I know you are weak." We are all forgiveness as far as the discipline of meditation is concerned. We forgive ourselves for our lack of effort yet we put no bridles on our anger towards the world.

It should be just the opposite. If we need to be angry, we should be angry towards our mind: "What are you doing to me?

Why are you trying to mislead me? Why are you making me waste my existence? Why don't you sit still and be quiet?"

Then there is greed. How many days do we spend in stores, shopping malls or online, purchasing all life's paraphernalia, accumulating it, savouring it, dressing ourselves up with it? We need the sharpest car and the best house. We need to see and be seen. These may seem like small things but soon, if we are not careful—filled with care for our soul—our mind will find there are skyscrapers we must own, empires we must create, whole populations we must milk for profit. To be content with just some knowledge becomes insufficient: we must know all things and amaze the world with our knowledge. The fact is that most of these things we don't need, so, basically, all this is nothing but greed and indulgence. But by the same token, are we greedy for meditation? Do we want more and more of it? No. When it comes to that, we become the embodiment of contentment. "I must lead a normal, balanced life; I can take only so much. I've done the most I can handle of meditation. I've gone to satsang; I'm content."

For the one who loves the Master, there is no such thing as contentment with meditation; there has got to be greed—insatiable greed. We always want more meditation, we always want more of the presence of the inner Master; there has got to be greed for that.

What, then, do we see if we analyze attachment? If we knew that someone were beating up a person we love, we wouldn't wait to get help. We would run and throw ourselves into the fray. Even if the person were much bigger than us, or there were twenty of them attacking, we would just ignore the fact and would flail around to protect this loved one whom we are attached to. Now when it comes to meditation, the soul, which is our real essence, is being molested, raped, beaten to death by the mind and senses, and yet, in the midst of that ordeal we manage to find detachment. "Oh, poor soul, this is your plight, the mind is powerful and I cannot defend you against it." We are very detached about the soul. "In the last moment the Master will come, like Superman, to the rescue. Don't worry. I do not need to make any effort. He will save you. He is attached to you."

Are we attached to our soul? It would appear that we are not. Rather, it would seem that we are very attached to the worldly things and unattached to that which is our essence. We say, "Oh, we have our children and our family and all that." It is true, we have all those relations, but who are they? The Master says this world is a play: many wives, many husbands, many children, through our many lives—we have had them all!

There is a story about a man who was very attached to his wife. When his wife died, he wanted a message taken to her, so he asked a spiritually advanced disciple to contact his wife. The advanced disciple went inside and then came back. The husband asked, "Well, what did she say?" The disciple replied, "She said, 'Who? Which husband? I've been with so many by that very name since I have been coming into this creation. To which husband are you referring?'" That is the extent of our attachments. We think these relationships are so real, so important, such vital obligations. With the spiritual perspective, however, we see we must reverse this way of thinking. It has to be just the opposite. Our priority has to be to consider our obligations to our soul. First and foremost, we have to value our soul so much that it is more important to us than everything else.

Then we come to the last of the five downward tendencies, which is ego. We think we are so valuable in this world that we should be recognized as important. We assume that people should want to be with us; that we should be paid more; that the

Master should come personally to thank us for 'our' seva, and so on. There is so much ego in us. Yet, when we come to the spiritual side of life, we become the embodiment of humility. Then, we are nothing. We become worthless. We can't fend for ourselves, and we can't battle against the mind. "Master, you have to do it for me. You have to meditate for me." We become all humility, and yet it should be just the opposite.

If there is anything that we need on this spiritual path to reach our destination, it is the determination of the ego. This may sound like a tremendous contradiction in the path because we are trying to eliminate the ego. The mind is so cunning it tries to cloud our clear thinking and we confuse the faculty of 'doing' with a negative association of 'ego'. At this stage on the spiritual path, firm resolve is more important to us than anything else, and a natural ingredient of ego is firm resolve. 'Firm resolve' is the determination to make things happen. 'Firm determination' is the quality of the mind that in Sanskrit is called *ahankar*, which also means ego and will power. It is this natural quality of the mind that becomes perverted when it gets out in the world and says, "I am this" and "This is mine". But in order to get to the eye focus we need this same quality to be directed to our advantage, so that it says, "I am going to do it, I am going to achieve it." If we don't have that faculty, we will never get to the eye centre.

Clear thinking on this matter is extremely important. In this plane, we are enmeshed in ego. It is through the ego that we function, and without it we cannot live. When it becomes time for us to do what is important for us to do, we have to *use* our ego. But the *use* of the ego is only a faculty, not an identity. When it comes to achieving something in this world such as getting a job, we exert our determination. When we go to school, we say,

"I can pass this exam. I can obtain this degree to get this job. I can succeed in this job." When we really want something, we go and get it. For our spiritual growth, we need to use that same determination.

In this way, we use the mind's natural behaviour to our advantage. The five 'sins' or 'passions' that stand in the way of spiritual growth are simply perversions of the mind's natural tendencies. We can take each of these passions and reverse them, transforming them from downward tendencies to positive powers, and create ballast for our upward journey. Lust, anger, greed, attachment, and ego can all be inverted to serve the spirit by supporting our meditation practice.

Unmasking the ego

> Within the body He Himself resides,
> Yet He cannot be seen, that Invisible One.
> Under the sway of mind,
> Fools know not the truth,
> And search for him outside.
>
> Guru Amar Das

Where there is thinking (mind), there is duality. Where there is duality, there is ego: "me and my thoughts" or "me and the world" or "I am one thing; the world is something else". Ego is sustained and fed by constant thinking. Ego cannot concern itself with living in the present, because being in the present threatens ego's very survival. Ego is kept alive by thinking constantly about the past or future. Without a past, it is hard to maintain an identity. Preoccupation with the future gives hope for the continued survival of ego. Ego is therefore always looking to get attached to some memory, situation or problem, to guarantee its survival and to reinforce its sense of self.

What ego fails to see is that this self is just a mask impersonating our real Self. Ego is the ignorance of who we really are. Ours is a case of mistaken identity. It is as if we were water contained in a glass bottle that is floating on the ocean, and we thought we were the bottle instead of the water. Eventually, the bottle will be smashed by the waves against the rocks and the glass will break. Once the bottle is broken, where is our separate identity? Where is the single drop? It doesn't exist any more. It has become the ocean.

> What has happened to me?
> I am now lost to myself!
> I look within me and I do not find myself.
> Within myself You abide.
> From head to foot You are there,
> And You too are within and without.
>   Bulleh Shah

When we die, we lose contact with our possessions and relations. Without these relationships with the outside world we will no longer be what we used to be, our ego will have no meaning, our personality as we experience it just now will have died with us. The word 'personality' derives from the Greek word 'prosøpeion', which means mask. This mask was used in ancient Greek theatre to portray a role or personality. Our ego is the mask, the personality or self we have built in this lifetime to cover our true Self. It is our 'false', our temporary identity, an impostor that pretends to be the real 'me'.

We will never become receptive to the truth of our own being until we unmask the ego, until the deceptive wall of duality between Shabd and the true self crumbles. The wall of ego that separates Shabd from us is made from the bricks we ourselves provide by indulging in thinking. Where there is thought there is ego. Where there is ego—'me' or 'you'—there is separation, impermanence and pain.

When one merges into the Absolute there is no ego, no duality, no separation and no pain. In the *Yoga Sutras*, Patanjali says that union is achieved through stillness of the thought waves. The only way one can merge back in the Absolute is by quieting the mind. This is very difficult to achieve but it is not impossible. By training the mind in simran, we control our thoughts and make them harmless. Then we are in a receptive state when we practise listening to the Shabd in bhajan. We go on practising our bhajan until we are able to hear the inner Sound. Once this is accomplished, we are drawn by the magnetic pull of the Sound. As our awareness of Shabd expands, ego occupies its proper place and the soul gains control. As the soul gains control, stilling the mind becomes a real possibility. Meditation is the means to still our mind, to become absorbed in the celestial music, to be bathed in the light of Shabd.

In answer to a fear expressed by many: we don't lose the sense of who we are by merging with the ocean of consciousness. On the contrary, we become who we really are, which is pure consciousness, perfect happiness, limitless love. What is this personality that we are so afraid to lose? What sense does it make that we remain satisfied with this dark world, separated from our true essence, when our possibilities are infinite? Let us become the ocean. Let us make the effort to avoid being bottled up again. Let us strive to merge back into Shabd. That is who we really are.

One day I wiped out all notions from my mind. I gave up
all desire. I discarded all the words with which I thought
and stayed in quietude. I felt a little queer—as if I were
being carried into something, or as if I were touching some
power unknown to me ... and ztt! I entered. I lost the
boundary of my physical body. I had my skin, of course,
but I felt I was standing in the centre of the cosmos. I spoke,
but my words had lost their meaning. I saw people coming
toward me, but all were the same man. All were myself!
I had never known this world. I had believed that I was
created, but now I must change my opinion: I was never
created; I was the cosmos; no individual Mr Sasaki existed.

                                        Zen Master Sasaki

It is the barrier of ego that prevents us from knowing our true
Self. By replacing self-centred thoughts with simran, by offering
our ego in meditation to the Master, the wall of duality will one
day crumble, the impostor will be unmasked, and we will gain
experience of who we truly are.

> When the desire for the Friend became real,
> All existence fell behind.
> The Beloved wasn't interested in my reasoning,
> I threw it away and became silent.
> The sanity I had been taught became a bore,
> It had to be ushered off.
> Insane, silent and in bliss,
> I spent my days with my head
> At the feet of my Beloved.
>
>   Shaikh Abu-Saeed Abil-Kheir

2

Priorities, attitude and effort

Seek ye first the kingdom of God
and every thing else shall be added unto you.

Matthew 6:21

What is it that we want?

Our true being is boundless. It has no limitations. But we have shifted our attention from that boundless absolute nature to the limited, relative, ordinary condition of our personalities. As long as we keep our attention away from our true nature, we will continue to live in duality, ignorant of the bliss that is within our reach. We waste our lives distracted by the world and its objects. Again and again, we fall under the material world's illusions and spells.

The Sufi mystic Rumi said that our situation is similar to that of a servant who is sent by a king to a country to accomplish a specific task. The servant goes to that country and does many wonderful and amazing things, and then returns to the king. Back at the king's court, the king asks him, "Did you do the task I sent you to do?" The servant answers, "My lord, please, first let me thank you. The place you sent me is a wonderful place. I met a beautiful lady and I married her. Then we had children and with them my responsibilities increased, so I opened a shop." The king interrupts him and says, "But what about the task that you were sent for? Did you or did you not perform that specific task? I didn't send you to get married, to have children, to make money or to get entangled in other types of affairs." The subject bends his head down in shame and says, "I am sorry, my lord, I forgot ..." The king replies, "How could you have forgotten the only thing you were sent to perform? You will have to go back and do it again." And that's how we keep coming back into this world.

As life goes on and as the years go by, we confuse our priorities as we get more and more distracted from our spiritual purpose by the affairs of the world. Soon we may no longer distinguish between what is essential and what is not. Meditation is essential. If we were to forget everything else and remember this one essential thing, then everything would be fine in our life. If we did a thousand other wonderful things and forgot this one essential thing, we would, at the end of our life, have done nothing whatsoever.

Meditation awakens us to the reality of our being. This should be our priority. We may hold a very important job . . . so what? We may have the best car ... so what? We may possess millions of dollars ... so what? We may have the best spouse and the most wonderful family ... so what? We may go on retreat, to an ashram, or to the Dera every year ... so what? We may see the physical form of the Master every day for the rest of our lives ... so what? Once we have been initiated, none of these can of themselves awaken us to the reality of our own true being. All of these are external aids and are at best a means to reach an end. Everything of real and lasting value that will be achieved will be achieved only by going within, through meditation.

Our lives reflect our priorities. Our actions speak louder than our words, for everything we do is done in accordance with our priorities. The time we get up, what we eat, what we think, what we do and what we abstain from doing, all stem from our priorities. By our actions, we determine our top priority, and this becomes the most important thing that we want in life.

If we choose to allow a pleasure-seeking society to brainwash us, our lives can easily become superficial and artificial, with priorities dictated by superficial and artificial needs. In today's commercial world, our likes, dislikes, fears and joys can easily become standardized by a society that wants to commodify everything, to turn us into consumer machines with material priorities and no connection with our spiritual lifeline.

We may not say it or even consider it, but by our actions are we demonstrating that acquisition or maintenance of material wealth is what we really want in life? Do we sometimes think that if we could only get that car, that computer, that job or house, then we would be happy forever and our lives would be complete? The fact is, and we know it, that once we obtain those objects, the day comes when we realize that having them does not satisfy us. Most people at some stage or other in their lives discover that making the acquisition of material things their priority leads to a degree of dissatisfaction, anxiety and depression—even when one attains whatever it was that was initially wanted.

We have only to look about us to see that wealth does not necessarily correlate with a sense of well-being; that having money or being poor has little to do with being happy or content. We all know of people who, in spite of having a lot of money, are miserable; we know of people who are poor but happy. We also know of rich people who are happy and of poor people who are unhappy. Is it not a person's level of contentment, their attitude to life, that makes the difference rather than the amount of wealth?

To know that enough is enough is to have always enough.

Tao Te Ching

If we believe that money is the answer to life's problems, we are likely to work ourselves into the ground at the cost of our spiritual life, and maybe our health, principles and families too. No matter how much we have in terms of material assets, these possessions do not translate into peace of mind. As disciples on the spiritual path, we need to bring ourselves to the point where we accept that what Shabd has given us, and the circumstances in which we have been placed, are the sum total of what we need to achieve as our life's goal.

The wise person, therefore, is the one who has reached a state of acceptance and contentment, and from there becomes desireless and joyfully serene. The secret to a happy and contented life is to learn to accept rather than expect. Acceptance and contentment are a fundamental part of the teachings of the Masters. They are not achieved through wishful thinking or mental affirmations. They are the natural outcome of a tranquil mind that is grounded in meditation.

If worldly priorities rank at the top of our list, we will never transcend our present condition and state of perpetual restlessness. With worldly priorities, meditation and the inner life will always come second. With worldly priorities, we will not experience the bliss that the Shabd Masters speak about.

Do not waste time uselessly. Be concerned about time spent in vain, and regret why so many breaths were wasted, since they were utilized neither in worldly affairs nor in spiritual pursuit.

Baba Jaimal Singh

Worldly priorities can contribute to making life comfortable in the world, but they will not fulfil our deepest yearnings. They will not fill our sense of emptiness. They will not take away our feeling of loneliness. When our priorities are worldly, we run away from facing our selves and from facing our loneliness, little realizing that this feeling is one of the greatest boons we have been granted.

> This constant feeling of loneliness and missing something is in reality the hidden unquenched thirst and craving of the soul for its Lord. It will always persist as long as the soul does not return to its ancient original home and meet its Lord. Only then will it get true contentment and eternal peace. This feeling has been purposefully put in the heart of man.
>
> Maharaj Charan Singh

Feeling lonely is the cry of the soul for its true home. It is the cry of our true Self to be given the space, the environment, the atmosphere in which it can feel at home. No amount of going places, keeping busy, entering new relationships, climbing the social ladder or buying more things is going to silence that cry. The only remedy is to give the soul what it craves by developing the habit of sitting daily for meditation.

> All the misfortunes of men derive from one single thing, which is their inability to be at ease in a room [alone].
>
> Pascal

If we want to get rid of our loneliness, anxieties and obsessions, we need to face our fear of being alone. We can help ourselves by asking some tough questions. What is it that we want in life? What is the pursuit of our present priorities doing to us? For what exactly do we work so hard? Are we compromising our ideals? Do we stay longer hours at work to earn extra money? If so, what is it we want to achieve? Why do we spend all that energy to enter that new relationship? Why do we waste our time in chat rooms or watching that late TV show? Is it really worth it?

We need to be rational and objective. Some logic and clear thinking needs to be there for us too! It is easy to waste our entire life in useless activities. Why are we so scared of facing ourselves? What are we running from? We work so hard to obtain perishable things: would we really invest everything we have in a business that we knew was doomed to failure? Who would put his or her energy or time into such a business? Yet, that is precisely what we are doing. It would be healthy and helpful for us to take a good look at all these things.

If we cultivate contentment irrespective of our position, activities and possessions, we will get much more out of life. Life is not meant to be spent frantically running from one place to another, full of tension and stress. Even animals lead more relaxed lives than many of us do. The danger is that from youth to old age we spend our time trying to make real our world of make-believe, but in the end, when our bubble bursts and we are faced with death, we wake up to the fact that we have nothing to show for all those priorities we pursued and cherished so much in life.

The realization of the deception of this drama comes only when we wake up—at the time of our death.

Maharaj Charan Singh

It is not wrong to have goals in life. The problem comes when we forget our real purpose. Balance between the material and the spiritual has to be there because the soul is housed in a body and its energy is channelled through the mind. Our trouble is that we overrate worldly pursuits and worldly satisfaction. In effect, we are obsessed. We lose sight of the fact that the material world can only bring us a lower and less permanent type of happiness, that in and of themselves material pursuits will never give us what we expect from them. It is important, therefore, to understand, with a spiritual perspective, the proper value of things and to act accordingly.

In order to set our priorities straight, we may imagine ourselves inverting the present direction of our mind. It is as easy to go up as it is to go down. We need to keep hammering on our mind to turn around, convincing it that it has to invert its apparently natural tendencies, look upwards and act on what our Master says.

To keep our priorities in perspective it is imperative that we choose to live the life of a true disciple. Meditation has to be at the top of our priorities. All other considerations have to come in second place. If something interferes with our meditation, we should discard it without thinking twice. As the German philosopher Goethe points out: "Things that matter most must never be at the mercy of things that matter least."

We need to realize that every time we sit for meditation, we are doing the most important thing a human being can do. Without meditation, we will continue to be part of the circle of birth and death. Once a true living Master has initiated us, there is nothing more important than meditation.

Put all your worries aside, because there is nothing higher than meditation. Increase the duration of your practice from day to day, never decrease it; always keep this in your mind.

Baba Jaimal Singh

Attitude: The all-important perspective

Nothing is true and nothing is false. All depends on the colour of the lens through which we look.

Ramon de Campoamor

Attitude is the point of view we apply to life. There is a connection between attitude and altitude. The higher our point of view or perspective, the more detached we become, and the better equipped we are to do our meditation. Meditation helps our attitude by giving us the altitude or cosmic perspective to see the big dramas of life as small or insignificant, rather than as gigantic, unsolvable problems. In turn, our attitude to meditation is a determining factor in the way our meditation will unfold. When we sit in meditation, we are training ourselves to operate from a perspective of accepting, letting go, being free. It is an attitude of obedience to a power we have accepted as greater than 'me'.

Our attitude in meditation should be to present ourselves to the inner Master, naked of purpose and agendas, with no expectations of results or inner visions. Putting aside all worries and desires, we release all preconceptions. With single-minded and gentle attention on the simran or to the Sound, we are to become receptive to the way of Shabd. In time, the patience, devotion, acceptance and surrender that we acquire in meditation will be transferred to daily life.

To live in that atmosphere is to live a simple, happy and relaxed life. The effect of that peace and bliss of meditation enables you to adjust according to the weather of life while retaining your equanimity and balance. You contentedly face your karmas, both good and bad, by continually adjusting to their ever-changing pattern. You can't change the course of events dictated by your destiny. But by obedience to the Master and by attending to meditation you remain happy and relaxed as you go through it.

Maharaj Charan Singh

We cannot force the growth of a tree we have planted. The tree has its own time to grow. Our job is to dig a hole, plant the seed, cover it with the soil, fertilize it, water it, protect it from pests and take care of it every day. That is the extent of our effort. The speed at which it grows is not up to us. If we have this attitude towards our meditation, we will not obstruct the Master's work and the tree of spirituality will undoubtedly grow and yield fruit in our lives. If we try to speed up the growth of the tree without first properly waiting for it to be rooted, then it can be torn up and destroyed by the winds of Kal's world. If we try to hurry, impose our expectations or force visions, then we will just be complicating the Master's work.

Our only concern is to keep our mind in simran at the eye centre, and to be receptive to the Sound. For that, and only that, are we responsible. It is for us to follow the instructions of Master and leave the rest to him. Whether results appear in our meditation or not, we will do well. Our part of the meditation is to keep our attention in the effort, not the results. The effort is up to us. The results are not.

In the *Tao Te Ching* we read: "Do your work, then withdraw. Such is the Way of heaven." And in the *Bhagavad Gita*, Lord Krishna advises his disciple Arjuna not to be concerned with results but only with actions. Then he goes on to say that the unwise cling to their actions, expecting results, while the wise perform actions for the Lord's sake, indifferent to results. Masters from all traditions emphasize the same point: Let go of results; effort is in our hands, results are not. If we are constant in our meditation practice, we will learn to become unattached to results. We will neither rejoice nor grieve when good or bad things happen to us. We will surrender and flow in harmony with the way of the Shabd.

Let us not worry about the problems of life! This, as disciples of a living Master, we can say to ourselves every day. The good and the bad things in life keep us attached to this creation. When we sit for meditation with a heavy heart, full of burdens and worries, it is difficult to bring our attention to the eye centre. When we take ourselves too seriously and do not know how to laugh at ourselves, we are only solidifying our ego and making life even more burdensome. If we use humour to make light of our load and laugh our problems away, we will sit for meditation with a relaxed and happy attitude and it will be easier for us to collect and focus our attention. For a disciple, the challenge is to cultivate an attitude of mind wherein we attend to all things of the world with a light heart, as a matter of duty, and no more.

Met with a positive attitude, this world can become a source of joy, inspiring us to see the divine will in everything and to worship the Lord through his creation. Expressing his overflowing sense of awe and gratefulness, the great Italian mystic Saint Francis of Assisi composed the *Canticle of the Sun* in praise of the Lord and all living creatures:

Most high, almighty, good Lord!
All praise, glory and honour belong to you!
Praise my Lord with all his creatures;
Especially for our Brother Sun,
Who brings us the day and the light;
Beautiful is he and he shines with such splendour,
That he reminds us of you, O Lord.
Praise my Lord for our Sister Moon, and for the stars,
Which he has set clear and lovely in heaven.
Praise my Lord for our Brother Wind,
And for the air and clouds;
And for every kind of weather
By which he nourishes all his creatures.
Praise my Lord, for our Sister Water,
Who is very helpful to us,
And humble and precious and chaste.
Praise my Lord, for our Brother Fire,
Through whom he gives us light in the darkness;
And he is beautiful and joyful and mighty and strong.
Praise my Lord for our Mother Earth,
Who sustains us and keeps us,
And brings forth herbs and diverse fruits
And flowers of many colours.
Praise my Lord for all those
Who pardon one another for His sake,
And who endure weakness and tribulation;
Blessed are they who shall in peace endure,
For by you, most high, shall they be crowned.
Praise my Lord for our Sister Death,
From whom no living man can flee.
Blessed are those who find themselves

> Living in your most holy will,
> For the second death will not reach them.
> Praise and bless my Lord, and give Him thanks,
> And always surrender to Him
> With great joy and humility.

A positive attitude gives us the ability to accept our condition and the inspiration to renew our commitment to meditation. With the right attitude, we look for the positive in everything and learn to identify ourselves with the Shabd in us and in all life forms. But most importantly, when doing meditation we keep focused on the effort. Then, whatever happens, we remain in balance and unaffected by the storms that are an inescapable part of the experience of being human.

> Let Him accomplish things in His own way rather than in the way that you desire. Try to adjust yourself to all that He does and you will never be unhappy.
>
> Maharaj Jagat Singh

Effort makes the difference

> It is the business and duty of every disciple to make his mind motionless and reach the eye centre. The duty of the Master is to help and guide on the path. *To control the mind and senses and open the tenth [inner] door depends on the disciple's efforts* ... The primary factor in this success is the effort of the disciple.
>
> Maharaj Sawan Singh

The moment we become initiated we receive all the grace we need to do our meditation. From there on, what counts is our effort. As Master Sawan Singh says in the quotation above, *we* have to control our mind, reach the eye centre and open the tenth door by our own effort. The Master will not do this work for us. We will go within only when we sit down for meditation and settle our thought waves at the eye centre. That is something only *we* can do.

If we want to achieve higher levels of spirituality, we must take action. We must take the steps that will lead us in that direction. Our actions must reflect our spiritual desire. If the desire for communion with Shabd is not reflected in our actions, either we are confused or we do not want to evolve spiritually. Our spiritual desire has to be expressed in the way we live, in the way we speak, in the way we think and adhere to the principles of the path. Most of all, it has to be expressed through our meditation. What would we think of a child who is late for school if he were to sit down in his house and pray, "O Lord! Let me not be late?" Wouldn't it be proper for the child that, while praying, he should also rely on his own effort and start walking in order to reduce the delay? Like the child, we also need to put in the effort, take action and make the best use of our time. In *Spiritual Gems*, Master Sawan Singh says:

> The Master is waiting inside for his pupils to come in and partake of his grace and love. It is our fault that we do not reach his 'feet' in the astral plane, above the eyes.

Once again, Master Sawan Singh is saying that it is up to us go within, that we are responsible if we don't reach his 'feet' (Radiant Form) in the astral planes.

What we are trying to accomplish is not easy. It requires a lot of effort. In the following text, inspired by Rumi, a description is given of what it takes to succeed in the spiritual life:

> Strive, struggle, grapple and wrestle,
> None won the battle by weak-kneed submission.
> Go on scratching, scraping and cutting
> The stone wall that bars your way.
> Cut, hew, gash, break, shatter, demolish, smash,
> Rest not for a second, till your very last breath arrives.
> Even a worthless effort is better than sleeping,
> For the Lord loves our effort, anxiety and struggle.
> First put in full effort, then accept what he sends.
> Have faith in him and trust his will.
> Not putting in effort is like sleeping among robbers.
> A bird found napping is sure to be killed.
> Giving up is like sleeping, sleep not on your way.
> March on until you reach his gate.
> When the Master has put a sword in your hands,
> He has clearly expressed his wish.

This sounds like a lot of work, and it is a fact. It is hard work! The spiritual way, to take the metaphor used by the Shabd Master Kabir, is not taking tea at auntie's house. Controlling the mind and senses is the most difficult thing to achieve on earth. We can make it less complicated or very difficult, depending on us. It is less complicated if we adapt the rest of our activities to it, if we make it our life's work. Then there are no difficult choices to make, no great sacrifices. But if we try to somehow squeeze Sant Mat into a lifestyle that's not compatible with it, we run into trouble. Then come the frustration and the discouragement, because it just doesn't seem to work.

Sant Mat teaching is very simple, but to follow it is much more difficult than it looks. It's a constant struggle with the mind, and one has to change one's entire way of life and one's attitude towards life. To follow Sant Mat requires a complete transformation, so it's not easy. One has to sacrifice a lot in life.

Maharaj Charan Singh

Master Charan Singh doesn't say that we have to make *some* sacrifices. He says we have to sacrifice *a lot*. If we really want to succeed, we need to adapt our lifestyle to Sant Mat and not Sant Mat to our lifestyle. We need to change our way of life according to the teachings, attend to our meditation and concentrate our attention at the eye centre. That is right effort, and that is what is expected from us. We cannot give up, believing that we can't meditate or that it is impossible to concentrate. We cannot afford to do that, not if we want to reach his gate. If we want to experience the true method of dying, if we want the ultimate benefit, our actions must reflect that desire.

We're not going to bring our attention to the eye centre and experience spiritual transport just by wishing for it. We have to work for it. The Master has expressed his wish by putting a sword in our hands. That sword is simran. We can wield it against laziness and lack of focus by persistence in doing simran. This will strengthen our resolve to sit and concentrate in meditation. We cannot afford the luxury of allowing procrastination and restlessness to stop us.

As we all know, a life of meditation is not easy. There are phases of struggle and periods of dryness. We should not let ourselves become unduly distressed by these phases. Feelings of being spiritually high are not the only indications of spiritual progress. We might even make more progress when our mind is restless, and in that distracted mindset we still sit for meditation. Moreover, if we pay too much attention to our laziness, lack of focus or restlessness, that very sense of inadequacy may persuade us to stay away from our spiritual practice.

Our best approach is simply to place firm faith in the Master and in ourselves that we will succeed. If we couldn't do it, he would never have initiated us. We have to put in all the effort on our part. Master Jagat Singh said in one of his satsangs: "Our prayers and pleadings are quite useless, unless these are supported by all the effort on our part to push the door open."

> *The first essential thing, therefore, is to enter this laboratory within ourselves, by bringing our scattered attention inside of the eye focus.* This is a slow process. But we are not justified in saying that we cannot do it, or that it is impossible, or that it is useless. Here is a worthy pursuit for the application of our critical and other faculties ... It is our job and we must do it; and we must do it now, in this very lifetime.
>
> Maharaj Sawan Singh

The first essential thing is to bring our attention to the eye centre. How do we do that? By concentrating on the words the Master gave us at the time of initiation. It may take us a long time to reach our goal, but continuous and constant effort is needed, as illustrated in the story of the tortoise and the hare and its moral—"slow and steady wins the race"!

The tortoise and the hare are going up a mountain, and the hare says, "I'm going to beat you hands down." He dashes off. Way out in front, he decides that he will lie down and take a rest, and in taking the rest, he falls asleep. Meanwhile, the tortoise is

laboriously moving along, very slowly, never stopping, and ultimately gets to the goal and wins the race.

Master Sawan Singh says: "This is a slow process." And
how does our mind interpret that? The mind interprets 'slow'
as meaning that it is going to take a long time for us to put in the
effort, but that is not what it means. What is slow is the process,
but the effort has to be extreme and without remission—extreme
beyond all measures—as in the story of the tortoise and the hare.
The tortoise has to make awesome effort because it has to carry
its entire existence with it. The progress is slow, but, because
the effort is big and without respite, in the end the goal is reached.

Master Sawan Singh has said that it is more valuable for us
to repeat the words and hold our attention at the eye centre than
to achieve anything else in the world. The mind doesn't think
that, nor does it appreciate our situation. The mind thinks, "Oh,
meditation is too hard, but I have a Master and I have nothing
to worry about because I have been initiated and everything has
been accomplished." This is not the case at all, for we are pris-
oners and we are trapped in an alien land. If we don't do our
part of the bargain, there is nothing the Master can do.

Our situation is desperate. We are being devoured by our desires and we are in imminent danger of reincarnating once again
as we lie back in this drunken stupor thinking that it is all too
hard. What is the use of making things harder for ourselves than
they already are? We should resume the journey. The sooner we
get back with full force on the Master's path, the happier we will
be. Why postpone the inevitable? Sooner or later we have to put
in the effort, so better do it now while we can. How do we succeed in anything in this world without applying time, attention
and effort? In meditation too, we have to apply that same time,
attention and effort, and only then it is possible to succeed.

The mind will come in and tell us that it is insane to do two and a half hours of meditation daily. This is just a trick of the mind. If we are willing to challenge it, we will find the mind is all bark and little bite. The Master has enjoined us to challenge it. We've got to say, "I have wasted enough of my life; I have wasted enough of this valuable treasure. The time has come to utilize this precious human form for its singular and most important purpose."

It is time to follow the Master's advice and take full advantage of the opportunity given to us. Now is when we give meaning to the word *action*. With our effort we show the Master that we care, and we become receptive and worthy of his grace. We can put in the effort to work towards the inner life by doing our meditation and devoting ourselves wholeheartedly to attain Self-realization; or we can commit half-heartedly and achieve half-hearted results. The choice is ours and ours alone. Grace is always there. Our effort is what makes the difference.

> If you take one step to take refuge in the Master,
> The Master meets you on the way
> By taking hundreds of steps.
> If you remember the Master just once,
> The Master remembers you again and again.
> Even if your devotion is as small
> As a fragment of a cowrie shell,
> The Master showers all benefits on you.
> The Master is all merciful,
> His praise is beyond understanding;
> I bow again and again
> To the one and incomprehensible Master.
>
> Bhai Gurdas

A practical approach to meditating two and a half hours daily

> The aim should always be to increase these periods [of
> meditation] gradually so that you can ultimately sit for two
> and a half hours at a stretch. There should be no hurry in
> doing so. Rather the progress should be consolidated.
>
> Maharaj Jagat Singh

If we have been initiated and we haven't been able to sit in meditation, or we started to sit but we stopped doing it, then we need
a practical approach to renew our commitment to sit for meditation. The important thing is to begin with what time we can.
Then gradually and persistently we can increase that time, not
jumping full-blown into two and a half hours for one or two
days then falling away to ten minutes or nothing at all. That is
not the way. The way is slow and steady: to increase the time
gradually.

We have to start from where we are, but we shouldn't kid
ourselves. Sitting for meditation will not happen automatically
on its own: we need to make it happen. For that we have to start
by making the time. Some sacrifices will have to be made, but
nothing is achieved without putting in time and effort, and that
time and effort will have to be taken from our daily schedule—
from things we are already doing. Maybe we will need to cut
down on our TV viewing time, or time in the chat room, or we
will have to get up earlier. Whatever it takes, it will be worth-
while. We need to take a good look at our daily schedule and see
when in the day we are going to make room for our formal sitting
time and for how long we will sit. After weighing work or family
responsibilities, we should then make our own schedule.

Unless we discipline our mind this much, our mind will always find excuses not to sit in meditation.

Maharaj Charan Singh

When we schedule our time for meditation, we should be practical about it. For instance, if our work starts at 8:00 a.m. and we want to meditate in the morning, at what time will we need to go to sleep at night in order to get up earlier? Will we get enough sleep? Maybe it would be best to consider doing our longer period of meditation at night.

If we get time in the morning, take advantage of it; if it is in the afternoon, meditate then; in the evening, then meditate in the evening. Whenever we sit in remembrance of the Beloved, our Friend—whether for a quarter of an hour, half an hour, one hour or two hours—it will be credited to our account and we will receive the benefit accordingly.

Maharaj Charan Singh

There may be days when it is physically impossible for us to meditate according to our plan. On those days, we should at least try to sit for some time. We shouldn't let a day go by in which we don't meditate, even if it is for just a few minutes. On the next day, we should resume our programme as usual. Otherwise, we might find that days, weeks, months or even years slip by without us meditating at all. It is crucial to create the habit. Even five minutes can make a difference in imprinting on our mind the desire to maintain our commitment. Master Sawan Singh used to say, "If you can't bring your success to me, bring your failures". We shouldn't become discouraged because we cannot sit for two and a half hours. Let us consolidate our progress as

we go, rather than feeling that it must be all at once or nothing
at all.

> If you force your mind to meditate and say, "Even if I can't
> give the proper time to meditation, let me give at least half
> the time, even if I'm busy," then you'll get regularity.
>
> Maharaj Charan Singh

Consider making a personal commitment to sit in meditation for one month at the same time every day. We could begin
by doing twenty or fifteen minutes a day. What matters most is
that we strengthen our will power and experience the fact that
we can do it. There is power in keeping a commitment, in knowing that our word is worth something. There is great value in
just making the commitment to meditate. We can set the alarm
to go off at whatever time we decide to meditate to make it easier
to keep our own personal commitment to sit at the same time
every day. When the alarm goes off, we sit. In this way, we will
begin to tread the path. At the end of the month, we might
choose to renew our commitment for another month, and then
again for another month—until we have established ourselves in
this habit. It is this, after all, which is going to bring us, ultimately,
the peace to conquer our restlessness and become masters of our
wayward mind and our untamed will. The important thing is to
build up the idea of a daily routine. After some time we will see
that the mind begins to look for the space to meditate, and, if for
some reason it doesn't find it, it will miss it.

To consolidate our habit, it would be best to keep ourselves
at a certain time limit after we have reached a specific goal. For
instance, if we started with fifteen minutes a day and we have
worked our time up to an hour, we might decide to stay there

for a period of at least six months to get truly established in that routine. Behavioural studies indicate that establishing a new habit takes from three to six months, so be patient! But keep in mind always to move forward with patient, single-minded tenacity, even if it takes years to reach the desired two and a half hours daily.

The journey of a thousand miles begins with a single step.
Tao Te Ching

It does not matter if we make plans that end up being unrealistic. Make new ones. Be prepared to go through a series of trials and errors. In the beginning, our most important goal is that meditation becomes part of our daily schedule. It is not important if we don't even manage to do a single round of simran in all the time we sit. What is important is that we have incorporated meditation into our lifestyle. Out of quantity, quality will come.

Many of us feel so restless that we cannot even sit for one minute in meditation. It is normal to feel restless and anxious when we try to control the wild beast of the mind. The fact that we cannot sit makes our need to sit all the more clear because through that we will start exercising some control over our mind. If now, when things in life may be going relatively well, we cannot control ourselves and stay seated for even a few minutes, then when conditions are bad, or we are sick, or dying, how will we be able to exercise the control needed to keep our attention at the eye centre so as to be receptive to the Master?

I am well aware that you have struggles. You have some things within yourself to overcome and some things outside

of yourself which must be surmounted. But you can do it.
If you have full confidence in the inner Master, he will
always help you. And often when you find the difficulties
greatest and the hour darkest, the light will appear and you
will see that you are free. Let nothing discourage you. This
is no light proposition, but your getting Nam means more
than if you had inherited a million dollars, or many millions. You are one of the lucky sons of Sat Purush, the true
Lord, and he has chosen you to get Nam and go with the
Master to Sach Khand, your true abode. You must reach
there. Nothing can prevent you. But you can hasten the
progress or retard it, as you like.

                                        Maharaj Sawan Singh

Sincerity and trying repeatedly will make a difference to our
motivation. Even if we have little motivation, effort is the place
to start. Motivation comes from what we value, and we naturally
stick with what is important to us. The knowledge that we are
doing what is best for our mind and soul should encourage us to
sustain our effort. This understanding will help us build the
motivation to make the effort to sit in meditation. Master Charan
Singh encourages us to do our best with the following loving
words:

> Do what you can as best you can, even if it is not deep and
> one-pointed. If you cannot find much time, if concentration
> is not attained and the mind wanders, do not be discouraged.

Through repeated action, we become stronger at what we
do. Even a small spark of determination will be enough to burn
to ashes all the limitations put on us by a mindset that refuses to

sit in meditation. Practice makes perfect. We should not worry if in the beginning we cannot concentrate in simran. What is important is that we stay seated for the time we predetermined.

Sometimes we give up at the slightest sign of discomfort. We should avoid this by forcing the body and mind to remain seated. The mind and the body will obey if we show determination. Expect them to move a lot, to complain a lot, to nag a lot. It is like a child's tantrum: if we hold the reins steady through simran, things will gradually calm down, and we will be able to enjoy the satisfaction that comes from being concentrated at the eye focus.

Restlessness, impatience and even pain can all be conquered. Look beyond their threat. See how they appear and disappear into nothingness. If success were immediate, then there would be no question of a fight. Practice means repeating the process over and over again. That's why it is called practice. That is the nature of the fight. That is all it entails.

Repeated effort and the Master's grace enable the mind to be conquered. It is time for us to jump into the circle of effort and grace. The more effort we put in, the more grace the Master showers on us. He initiated us because he knows that we can become conscious of our true Shabd Self. He knows we can become conscious of who we really are because, at a deeper level, there is no difference between us and him. We are all Shabd beings going through the experience of being human.

> Our deepest fear is not that we are inadequate.
> Our deepest fear is that we are powerful
> Beyond measure.
> It is our light, not our darkness that most frightens us.
> We ask ourselves, who am I to be brilliant,

Gorgeous, talented and fabulous?
Actually, who are you not to be?
You are a child of God.
Your playing small doesn't serve the world.
There's nothing enlightened about shrinking,
So that other people won't feel insecure around you.
We were born to make manifest
The glory of God that is within us.
It's not just in some of us; it's in everyone.
And as we let our light shine,
We unconsciously give other people permission
To do the same.

Marianne Williamson

There are disciples who couldn't even sit for one minute who are now doing more than two and a half hours daily. If others have done it, so can we. Everyone has responsibilities and busy schedules, yet there are some who manage to find three or four hours daily for their practice. And remember, these are often people who earlier couldn't sit for a single minute. They too felt that they would never be able to sit, but they showed courage and determination, and they succeeded, like all of us can. Because they had a will, they found a way. Because they had determination and showed that they cared, their Master took them through the obstacles. This is the faith we must have.

But Jesus beheld them, and said unto them,
With men this is impossible; but with God all things are possible.

Matthew 19:26

We should always keep our objective in front of us, bearing in mind that to meditate two and a half hours a day is not an arbitrary length of time chosen at random by the Master. This ten percent of our daily time dedicated to stilling our mind at the eye centre is the minimum required to break through the surface level of ordinary consciousness to a deeper level within ourselves. Even if we devote a small time to meditation, we will increase our will power and experience relaxation, a sense of well-being and an increased feeling of strength to face the world while holding on to our spiritual objective.

If we are sincere, and we give as much time as we can give, that will be enough to strengthen our spiritual heart and to kindle the flame of devotion that will take us, in time, to reach our goal of meditating two and a half hours daily. In the end, all our endeavours help us grow in love and devotion. The practice of meditation is nothing but the way to true devotion. However softly we call on him, he is always there for us.

> You just call out my name
> And you know wherever I am
> I'll come runnin'
> To see you again.
> Winter, spring, summer or fall
> All you have to do is call
> And I'll be there.
> You've got a friend.
>
>   Carole King

3

Meditation is a way of life

Meditation is a way of life. You do not merely close
yourself in a room for a few hours, then forget about
meditation for the rest of the day. It must take on a
practical form, reflecting in every daily action and in
your whole routine. That itself is an effect of medita-
tion. To live in the teachings, to live in that atmosphere
is itself a meditation. You are building that atmosphere
every moment for your daily meditation. Everything
you do must consciously prepare you for the next medi-
tation. So meditation becomes a way of life, as we live
in the atmosphere we build with meditation.

Maharaj Charan Singh

Meditation finds expression in the way we live. With meditation, our positive qualities begin to show. Tranquillity replaces
anger, contentment replaces greed, devotion replaces lust, humility replaces ego, and detached lovingkindness to all replaces
attachment and self-centredness. With meditation we are more
focused, more skilful and more productive in anything we do. We
naturally adjust our priorities and behave in a manner that is in
harmony with the inner Self and with our external surroundings.

If in everything we do, we live consciously in the atmosphere
created by meditation, then meditation becomes our way of life.

In the beginning, our meditation may seem divorced from our daily life. It is like two people who live in the same house and do not talk to each other. In time, daily life and meditation become integrated and support each other. From meditation we learn to be present, more concentrated, more generous, in whatever we do throughout the day. The attitudes of surrender, patience, contentment and awareness that are strengthened through the process of meditation are naturally applied to every aspect of daily life. Our lives then reflect the peace, joy and calmness that develop automatically through the practice of meditation.

Meditation helps us to see how there is oneness between everything and everybody in the creation—that, externally and internally, all is Shabd. We see how everything is interconnected. As we bring this realization to all aspects of our daily life, we demolish the walls we have built that separate our spiritual life from our daily life. The fracture that is experienced by so many people in the wholeness of their being is gradually healed.

If we analyze our tendency to see our meditation as separate from our daily life, we will understand that it is simply a symptom of this fracture, or fragmentation, that we typically experience in many aspects of our lives. What we say is different from what we do. Our spiritual desires are not reflected in our actions. We are in one place but wish we were in another. We are doing one thing but thinking of doing something else. Since we are never in the present and never being where we are, it's no wonder that meditation seems so boring: we are never there. And yet meditation is the only remedy for this fragmentation, this cosmic fracture that has not only separated us from God and the Master, but has also torn apart our inner being.

Live in the moment

Life is what happens to you while you're busy making other plans.

John Lennon

One of the most famous discourses Buddha gave was when he sat to give his speech to the sangat, and without uttering a single word, he just raised a flower in his hand. He held it there for a moment, and then he left. That was all he had to say. Only one among the thousands that had gathered to hear him understood the profound hidden meaning of his gesture. On realizing it, he became enlightened.

Buddha was teaching that all we have is this moment. In this moment, everything is perfect. There are no creations of the mind, no problems—just awareness of this flower in the stillness of the mind. Outside the moment, life is suffering. Our suffering is the result of the desires and cravings that spring from dwelling in the past and projecting problems and scenarios into the future. Baba Ji says that our problems are such because we choose to perceive them that way. The problems lie in our mind, in the way we think, not in the things themselves. Jesus used to tell his disciples to stop asking: What will we wear? What will we eat? He advised them to observe how the flowers and the birds live in the moment and how all their needs are taken care of. He would say: Ask yourselves how anxious thought can add even the slightest measure to your life! All experts on spirituality have said the same: All we have is this moment.

View'd from eternity, existence is simultaneous.
View'd from time, existence is successive;
The past and the future are in the NOW of eternity.

The consciousness of life in eternity's *At Once*
Is infinitely fuller
Than in the finite succession of time.

Clemens Humilis

If we keep our attention in the present moment, our problems shrink for lack of sustenance and we naturally, automatically, lead a happier life. Meditation is an exercise in being here, now. When we live in the present, we become fully alive as our consciousness reaches out far beyond the limitations of our ego. Ego exists through this very avoidance of being in the present— in its own realm of mental make-believe. By remembering the past and projecting into the future, by dwelling on our problems and desires through our habit of compulsive thinking, we feed and strengthen our ego. On the other hand, the more we stay in the present, the more the ego and all its accompanying problems wither away. Practising meditation and simran throughout the day is the easy way to keep our attention in the now, as well as a sure way to spare ourselves from unnecessary mental projections that bring us miseries and worries.

The present moment is the most valuable thing there is. Nothing happens tomorrow, nothing happens yesterday, everything always happens *now*. In fact, the 'now' is the only *time* there is. It is impossible for us to do or to think something outside the present moment. When we remember, it is always in the *now*. When we think about the future, it is always in the *now*. When the future catches up, it is always in the present moment.

By helping us to become still, present, and concentrated in the *now*, meditation is a great training. By keeping our attention in simran throughout the day, we eliminate our ego's need to inflate its importance by living constantly off memories of the past or off fears for the future. When our attention is in the now, it is difficult for us to be trapped by our own mind. With the practice of meditation and simran throughout the day, we become able to hold the focus of our consciousness in the now. We transcend the limitations of our ego and we enjoy our life from moment to moment. Living in the moment, being fully present in our own life, we are empowered to become serene witnesses of our own lives while we engage with and fulfil our responsibilities.

There is something wrong with us. We never want to be happy at the present moment. Either we are worried about what we have done or about what is going to happen to us. We don't want to make the best use of the present moment. If we make this moment happy, our past automatically becomes happy, and we have no time to worry about the future. So we must take life as it comes and spend it happily. Every moment should be spent happily. And simran helps.

Maharaj Charan Singh

True seva

All work is his work; remain happy wherever he keeps you, and take on whatever work you do as the Satguru's work.

Baba Jaimal Singh

As we practise meditation, the depth of our desire to realize or to experience the fullness of this human opportunity that we are going through will naturally be reflected in our actions. The reality of spiritual progress is first measured not by inner experiences, but by increasing levels of serenity and contentment, by acceptance of one's karmas or destiny, and by how we behave when in contact with our fellow human beings. Are we now kinder, more helpful, more tolerant than before we were initiated? Are we only interested in inner experiences or do we have a growing sense of the extraordinary experience to be had simply in the effort of being truly compassionate to others, in the work of becoming true human beings? The practice of meditation will naturally find expression in the details of daily life and in the way we relate to others.

> No man is an island, entire of itself; every man is a piece of the Continent, a part of the main.
>
> John Donne

Baba Ji says that we don't serve or help others in order to deepen our spiritual life; it is the other way around. The deepening of our meditation practice naturally develops in us the desire to be helpful to others. This desire finds its natural expression in the disposition to serve. Seva is service to the Master through service to our fellow human beings. Nobody is being more helped than the one who does the service. The purpose of seva is to help us expand in our love. Seva is an act of love meant simply to help us grow in love. That is seva. The practice of meditation will gradually help us to look upon everything we do as the Master's work.

The worldly obligations you are fulfilling are all essentially spiritual. Do not allow the self to intrude; everything is the Satguru's work.

Baba Jaimal Singh

Outward seva helps us to be more humble and receptive by taking the focus away from the 'me'—from our self-centredness. Seva is a way of expressing our devotion, and it is done in a spirit of gratefulness and humility, with total disregard for gain or recognition and irrespective of whether it is the sangat or our community in general that we serve. If it reinforces the ego, it is not seva and we should leave it.

Our most important seva is to attend to our meditation. No amount of outward seva can be a substitute for meditation. If we do outward seva at the cost of meditation, then we should abandon that seva. The reason we do seva is to create a spiritualized atmosphere in which to live our lives, to condition the mind to an atmosphere of spirituality so that it becomes easier for us to do our meditation.

Withdrawing our consciousness to the eye centre and connecting it with the Sound is the real seva ... Some people give emphasis only to the means without worrying about the end, which is wrong. We clean a cup or a utensil not to see it clean, but because we want to use it.

Maharaj Charan Singh

The joy and benefits of meditation

Having once contacted it, we find that Sound Current so fascinating, so charming and tempting, so captivating, that immediately we become attached to it, and automatically we become detached from the senses.

Maharaj Charan Singh

As our practice of meditation matures, and as we experience through it a quiet mind, we taste real rest and joy. We become less interested in running after external satisfactions and voluntarily go back to the restful and joyful place the mind has found within. With the successful practice of meditation, we experience for ourselves the fact that meditation is more valuable than money, greater than power, more sublime than sex, more satisfying than any favourite food or drink and more rewarding than anything else the mind has experienced. Baba Ji tells us that nothing in this world can come close to experiencing the Sound Current, that meditation is the ultimate pleasure, and that once we have had a taste of it we want more and more.

The happiness Baba Ji is referring to is not on the level of feeling, emotion or sensation. Rather the Master is referring to a higher level of joy that, at its highest, is defined by absolute freedom from relationships, objects, worldly joys, delusions and other external conditions. He is referring to the ecstatic bliss that is to be discovered when we go deep within our consciousness, where the Sound Current is constantly reverberating.

Once the mind becomes fond of listening to this 'voice of God', it turns away forever from the world and all worldly objects. The sweetness of this inner spiritual melody makes everything else seem tasteless or bitter. Compared with its enchantment, everything else seems dull and uninteresting. The possession of diamonds naturally causes one to lose interest in coloured shells. In the same way, the sweetness of the inner melody makes this world cease to be an attraction and turns the mind Godwards. One's love for the world comes to an end and love for God takes its place.

Maharaj Charan Singh

At the same time that meditation brings us closer to our goal of realizing our true nature, it also provides notable emotional, physical and health benefits. Because meditation is our primary way of loving the divine, when we meditate and increase our love, this leads to perceiving the divine in all things and loving the creation. Meditation helps us become more human, more loving, compassionate and peaceful. Focusing our attention in meditation improves our ability to concentrate and relax. This improved concentration and relaxation can be applied not only in meditation, but also in anything we choose to do, so that our ability to participate effectively in life improves.

Even Western scientists have become interested in the positive psychological and physiological effects of the many different practices of meditation. Since the 1960s there has been an increasing volume of research on the health benefits of this inner work. Physicians frequently recommend some form of meditation to help with a variety of stress-related conditions and many companies encourage their staff to practise meditation. People who meditate generally manage stress better, which reduces time lost for sick leave and leads to improved productivity and staff morale. This is because reduced stress improves the way the body functions and the way we feel about what we do.

Meditation has also become a common prescription for patients with high blood pressure and heart disease. The reason for this is simple. Medical science has proven that since meditation reduces stress and increases relaxation, it helps heart patients lower their blood pressure and improve the function of their cardiovascular system. In addition, it has been shown that when patients undergo surgery and different forms of medical treatment such as chemotherapy, a meditation practice can reduce a patient's recovery time and increase the positive outcomes of the traditional medical treatment.

However extraordinary the physiological and psychological benefits of meditation are, it is the spiritual benefits of meditation that are beyond all measure. Through the Masters, we learn that meditation is the way to empower our soul and purify ourselves of countless karmas. Meditation is the supreme way to surrender the ego, to accept the way of Shabd, and to transcend mental realms so that we can experience our deeper spiritual nature. Through our efforts in meditation, we give expression to our deepest yearning for self-knowledge and union. Meditation is the one prayer that is pleasing to the Lord; it is the one means to experience and merge with our source. Through realization of the Self, ultimately we attain realization of the divine.

> We should not be seeking consolation from this practice, but let us do it motivated by love and because God wishes it.
>
> Brother Lawrence

Meditation is the best way to prepare for death

Meditation is nothing but a preparation to leave the body. That is the real purpose of meditation. Before you play your part on stage, you rehearse the part so many times, just to be perfect. Similarly, this meditation is a daily rehearsal to die, so that we become perfect at how to die and when to die.

Maharaj Charan Singh

At the time of death, the concentration gained in meditation will give strength and direction to our mind and soul. The mystics reveal to us that through meditation it is possible to conquer death. Hence, Saint Paul says: "I die daily," and Rumi encourages us to practise in the following words:

> What a blessing it would be
> If you were one night to bring your soul out of the body,
> And, leaving this tomb behind,
> Ascend to the skies within.
> If your soul were to vacate your body,
> You would be saved from the sword of Death:
> You would enter a Garden that knows no autumn.

Keeping our attention at the eye centre is the first step to enable us to master the practice of dying while living. Besides our appointed time of meditation, we can practise keeping our attention at the eye centre at all times. It is especially helpful to us if we practise this at moments that resemble the time of death, when everything seems chaotic or out of our control. This may be when we are angry or possessive, when we are experiencing pain or suffering, or when we want to control events that are not in our hands. All these moments present to us excellent opportunities to learn to be detached, to let go and to concentrate our attention at the eye centre by means of simran.

Such training and self-discipline will prove invaluable at the time of death. It will also help us practically, so that we become more carefree and at peace with ourselves while we live our daily life. If we are able to make a habit of keeping our attention in the remembrance of our Master in all situations, then, when death comes, our attention will only be on our Master. This is extremely important because whatever we think about at the time of our death will determine the direction in which the soul goes after death.

> Whatever the state of mind
> That a man may focus upon
> At the end, when he leaves his body,
> To that state of mind he will go.
>
> Bhagavad Gita

If during our life we haven't trained our mind to be at the eye centre and we have only craved for the things of the world, death will not change those cravings. The impressions of the mind will still be with us at the time of death. The desire to be back with loved ones or to continue to experience worldly pleasures may be so strong that we will be pulled back into another birth to fulfil that very desire.

Imagine the situation of a person who one day goes for lunch in a restaurant, and when he comes out finds that someone has stolen his car. He then walks back to work, only to find that his place of employment has closed down and his bank account is empty. Full of anguish, he returns home, only to learn that his house has burned to the ground and all his loved ones have perished in this tragic incident. We may shake our heads in disbelief at the possibility of something so far-fetched actually happening to anyone. Yet, this is what each of us will experience at the time of our death. In one stroke, in one moment, we lose all our possessions, all we have and everyone we love.

If we haven't prepared beforehand, we may be devastated. If we die with a feeling of anguish and loss, of longing for what we are leaving behind, death will be a terrible experience. In the midst of holding on to dear life, how could we possibly welcome death?

We are mistaken if we think that by attending satsang, reading Sant Mat literature, having the Master's physical darshan and occasionally doing our meditation, we will be prepared to accept such an event with dignity and peace. Rather, we have to take advantage now of the opportunity to meditate, and train our mind to remain steady at the eye centre. Let's not be under any illusions. During this very life, we must attend to daily meditation. Then, and only then, will we be able to take refuge at the eye centre at the time of death and peacefully and willingly accept what is happening to us.

Meditation is the single most practical thing we can do to prepare ourselves for what we will experience when we leave the physical world at the time of death. If we are successful in keeping our attention at the eye centre for prolonged periods of time in meditation, we will go within and experience what it is to die, while living. Death will then hold no mystery for us. Instead of being a frightening experience, it will become something we anticipate, something full of wonder, beauty and promise—something to look forward to, something we know.

Die to live. You must withdraw to the eye centre, and then you will live forever. Otherwise, you are just living to die. Every time you live, you have to die, so die to live. Learn to die so that you may begin to live, and live forever.

Maharaj Charan Singh

For those who learn to die through the practice of meditation, death is not terrifying because they have traced each step in the process of death. Such disciples are receptive to the Master and remain conscious and confident during the experience, accepting it peacefully and without anxiety, regrets or fear. Keeping our attention in the eye focus cannot be overemphasized. It will prove invaluable at the time of death, but also while we are alive. Such is the power of meditation—for living, for dying, and for taking us on a journey beyond body and mind.

> Your breath is like a drumbeat,
> Constantly proclaiming the departure
> Of the caravan of life.
> Radha Soami has docked his ship –
> Come on board and cross the ocean free of charge.
>
> Soami Ji Maharaj

4

The source of love and devotion

Were it not for His grace, we would never even
think of our separation from Him, nor would we
desire to return Home. But for His grace, we would
neither meet the Master nor follow the Path.

Maharaj Charan Singh

Our past positive actions through many lifetimes and the grace of Shabd have brought us into the presence of a living Master. Since the time of our birth, the Master has been with us. He is our true companion. Whenever we have been in sorrow or despair, at the lowest points in our life, the Master has been there, waiting for us to realize the illusion in which we exist.

> The Master not only guides and helps during the disciple's lifetime, but stays with him even at the time of his death, and afterwards.
>
> Maharaj Charan Singh

The living Master is our link with Truth. Baba Ji says, however, that it is important that we question and inquire about all aspects of the teachings. He frequently points out the need for us first to relate to the teachings and find them logical and truthful; otherwise we will not be able to do justice to the teachings or to the Master. Having our doubts resolved will give us the necessary confidence and trust that we are on the right path, with the right teacher. This trust will help us remain constant in our meditation, and our constancy, in turn, will give us the balance and equanimity that support spiritual growth.

It is for us to find within ourselves the tenacity and endurance to follow the Master's teachings to the end, bearing in mind that it is the truth of his teachings that is important, not his personality. It is important that we don't become blinded by his appearance and lose sight of the fact that the true Master is Shabd.

Our real Master is the Word, the Logos, Shabd, Nam, the Audible Life Stream or whatever name one may choose to give it. The Master is that Power manifested in human form.

Maharaj Charan Singh

Since the Master is the human manifestation of Shabd, and we too are part of Shabd, when we meet the physical Master he seems very familiar. We may feel we have known him forever or that we have met before. In reality, at a deeper spiritual level, he is us. How can anyone be more closely connected to us? He is our own true Self. The only difference is that the physical Master is aware that his real form is that of Shabd while we are not aware of this truth. With the constant practice of meditation, the layers of misconceptions and illusions that cloud our perception begin to dissolve, and we start to see that the outer and inner Masters are one and the same.

He that hath seen me hath seen the Father.

John 14:9

As we gradually become aware of the connection between the disciple's identity and that of the Master, an indescribable bliss, gratitude and devotion are born in us. Through the deepening of our meditation practice, this feeling of devotion increases until we go deep enough to realize that Shabd, Master and disciple are one and the same.

> Within me the Father has revealed Himself;
> Father and son have met and become one.
>   Guru Arjun

Meditation is devotion

> You can build love and devotion only through meditation, not otherwise. Meditation builds everlasting love.
>   Maharaj Charan Singh

Love is the fruit of devotion. Meditation is the way to kindle devotion. Meditation is where we find the depth of love. Meditation will build within us the true devotion that will take us to the heart and the source of Shabd, to the home of the Master of our soul, to our Radha Soami. Without devotion, we are as the living dead; without longing, we are barren and a desert. The way to kindle longing for this love is through meditation, for devotion finds its fullest expression when we surrender our whole being to the Master, through giving ourselves to Shabd in meditation.

> The only way to strengthen love is by meditation. There's no other way, because the love which we get by experience cannot be compared to any other type of love.
>   Maharaj Charan Singh

It is only through meditation that absolute or ultimate Truth is realized. Truth, or Shabd, cannot be realized by logic or by intellect. The path of the intellect does not take us beyond the realm of the mind. The way to go beyond the mind and to gain access to direct perception or the spiritual experience of reality is by stopping the currents of thought through the practice of meditation, with love and devotion.

The heart has its reasons which reason knows nothing of.

Pascal

Devotion is a practical way to become receptive to the teachings of the Masters. If we see the Master as a teacher of logic and intellect, then we will get words and explanations. If we try to know the Master as he really is, without the hindrance of the intellect, then we will come to know him as the embodiment of Shabd. For those who are intellectual by nature, this is very difficult to do, but we need to start somewhere. However artificial and stone-hearted we may have become, raised as most of us have been on scientific materialism, we still yearn to experience feelings of love, awe and longing, like those recorded by the lovers of Shabd.

Love came and emptied me of self,
Every vein and every pore
Made into a container to be filled by the Beloved.
Of me, only a name is left,
The rest is You my Friend, my Beloved.

Shaikh Abu-Saeed Abil-Kheir

The path of devotion or *bhakti* can begin by simply recognizing the Master's kindness, by not taking him for granted. The spark of longing, and receptivity to his love, can be ignited by gratitude—gratitude to the Master for giving us initiation, for teaching us to meditate, for teaching us what to do with our mind and how to live our life; gratitude for putting us on the right path, for giving purpose and direction to our life, for teaching us, by his example, to love beyond our self without thought of reward. As we look back on the time before he called us to him, we will remember with gratitude the many things done for us even then to transform, and spiritualize, our life.

A time will come when we will see our Master as something more than a mere human being. When, through meditation, we are able to relate to him as the embodiment of Shabd, we will be able to receive the full transforming and purifying power of his teachings. This receptivity we will only get from meditation. Without meditation, we will be able to perceive only a fraction of a fraction of his love and wisdom. That is why it is so important that we try to develop the highest type of devotion through meditation, not confusing emotion with devotion.

Emotion, rightly directed, becomes devotion

> Emotions are all right if they lead you to devotion, but they should be channelled. If you let loose your emotions, they become a nuisance. If the river flows within its banks, only then it is useful. But when the river floods, it overflows its banks and creates devastation everywhere.
>
> Maharaj Charan Singh

The mind wants us to believe that the path of devotion is one of romance, and it entices us to think, "Here is the Beloved. I am going to merge in him. He is always the father looking after my needs. I don't have to put in any effort. He is taking me to Sach Khand, and all will be wonderful." This is pure deception of the mind. All saints have told us that the path of love is a path of struggle.

The lovers of the Lord go into the battlefield with their heads on the palms of their hands. This is how they find the Beloved. No one has found the Shabd through emotional excitement. To paraphrase a quotation from Kabir: When the celestial war drum is beaten, the warrior rushes forth to battle; bare-chested, he fights without weapons. The coward, on the other hand, slinks away, turns on the TV, calls someone on the phone, enters a chat room, visits friends, loses himself in indulging the senses, and thinks a thousand thoughts, with his mind darting in every direction. The last thing he wants is to have to face the battle.

The battle is inside, and it is inside that it has to be fought. The war drum is beating constantly, calling us to arms. This fight is the real purpose of our life. This is what is essential for us now. In practical terms, it means to keep our attention as much as we can in simran, at the eye centre. This is the way of the spiritual warrior, the way to empower the soul, the essence of the path of devotion, the foundation for a more mature relationship with our Master.

The strongest warrior is he who conquers himself.

Aztec saying

True devotion is to keep our attention at the eye centre. If we feel devotion, but cannot concentrate our attention at the eye centre, we may be confusing emotion with devotion. Unfocused emotion scatters the attention and dissipates precious energy.

It is the concentration of our attention, of all our longing and consciousness, at the eye centre, that alone will enable us to break through the barrier of the physical. This alone will bring us into contact with the inner experience that will enable us to sustain true longing and devotion. This inner experience cannot be had if our attention is scattered and misdirected outwards by emotion. That is why devotion is not the same as emotional excitement. It is important to distinguish between the two.

> Love is always within. When you try to dramatize your love, you lose the depth of the love.
>
> Maharaj Charan Singh

Sant Mat, the path and practice of the saints, is not a matter of lip service or emotional excitement. It is a profound way of life to be lived, within ourselves, at every moment and at every level. The mind falls into the trap of wanting to run after the physical form of the Master because it believes that this is the way to demonstrate love for him. We get caught up in running after the physical form of the Master like going to see a rock 'n' roll star. Everybody is jumping up and yelling, and because of all the emotional excitement buzzing and humming around us, we soon find ourselves jumping up and yelling too. We may ask ourselves why this so often happens in the relationship of spiritual Master and disciple.

Could it be because we want to believe that running after the physical form of the Master will give us spiritual benefit to compensate for our lack of effort in meditation? Could it be that we cannot face the effort required of us to go beyond the physical level to discover Truth? We want the easy way out. But the fact is that no amount of seeing the physical form of the Master will compensate for a lack of meditation. And when we put the Master on a pedestal and worship him in his physical form, are we not treating him like a stone idol, an image of what is already an image of Truth? Taking an analogy that Master Charan Singh often used, it is like the sun reflecting on water that is then reflected on a wall. Rather than being content with the reflection on the wall, would we not do better to seek to see the sun itself?

> People think that by running after me or by greeting me and saying 'Radha Soami' many times, they will get spiritual benefit. It is nothing but their own deception. What do they get out of it? By touching my hand or my clothes or putting the dust from where I have walked on their forehead, they get nothing.
>
> Maharaj Charan Singh

When we confuse emotion with devotion and follow blindly our own need for outward rituals and tangible evidence, when we give up the spiritual fight and surrender to our human tendency to ritualize and reduce everything to the physical, we are doing a great disservice to the Masters and their teachings. We are being deceived by our mind. True devotion is trying to please the Master by bringing our attention up to the eye centre. To help him in his promise to liberate our soul is the greatest demonstration of love we can give him.

> Running after the physical form of the Master is something very different from having love for the Master.
>
> Maharaj Charan Singh

The task of the physical form is to initiate us and to introduce us to the inner Master. The Master has told us where his real form is. Now it is up to us to pursue it. The physical is a means, not an end. We need the physical to love because we cannot develop the love needed for success on the spiritual path if its object is just an idea, a concept, in our mind. Our aim has to be to direct our love for the outer Master into effort in meditation so that we reach beyond the physical to the spiritual.

Let us not get so attached to the physical form that we stop our efforts to see him within. Buddhist Masters express this dramatically by saying: "If on the road you find Buddha, kill him." Here they are not talking about the physical—not that we have to physically kill the Master, but we have to 'kill' our limited concepts. They are trying to provoke us out of our slumber by drawing our attention in such a dramatic fashion to our limitations. We are ignorant of who the Master is. As we grow in understanding of the purpose of the physical Master, we cannot stop there. We must carry on our search for the Master's real form—the Shabd form.

> Nevertheless I tell you the truth; It is expedient for you that
> I go away: for if I go not away, the Comforter will not come
> unto you; but if I depart, I will send him to you.
>
> *John* 16:7

Commenting on this quote, Shabd Master Charan Singh writes: "He [Jesus] says: When I leave you, it will be in your interest. Hearing this, the disciple is surprised. How can it be in the interest of a disciple that the Master leave him physically? Christ explains: Day and night you are running after me now. You are mad in your love, and you are not trying to devote your time to the Spirit inside. But without attaching yourself to the Comforter, the Holy Ghost, you can never go back to the Father. So when I leave you physically, you will not find me anywhere outside and you will have no option but to seek me within. Then you will be in touch with the Comforter, who will pull you up to my level, the level of the Father."

In the introduction to the book *Nobody, Son of Nobody*, a story is told of a young disciple whose Master has turned cold towards him and finally has him thrown out of his presence. Bereft and in anguish, with no one else to go to, he turns to the Lord and throws himself on his mercy. Suddenly an indescribable peace descends upon him and he tastes that which he was seeking. At that moment his Master comes to him, and still confounded, the disciple asks him how he could treat him that way. The Master answers, "You had given up all and everyone, but there was still someone between you and your Lord; me! I was the only idol left in the temple of your hopes, wants and fears and that had to be taken from you for your ego to surrender and take refuge in the Beloved. Rise now, let's relish this victory."

All Masters proclaim the same truth. The true Master is Shabd. True darshan is inner darshan. The Truth is within. The journey of Sant Mat can take the disciple to the innermost level of Truth, but the disciple has to travel there. The Master can point to Truth, but he cannot experience Truth for us. A father has done his job when his sons and daughters are no longer dependent on him. It is only then that the father becomes happy, because he has accomplished his fundamental task of bringing the children up. Likewise, the task of the living Master is to show us how to make contact with the Radiant Form so we can gradually distinguish true from false and travel the path with firmer and stronger steps.

The true Master is the Shabd that projects itself into a human form and descends to the physical level, disguised as a human Master, to introduce us to the Master within and to bring us back to our source. A mature level of devotion is one where the disciple realizes that the true Master is the Master that never dies. Meditation is the way. Meditation is the means by which the love and natural emotions generated by contact with one who lives by Truth are directed inwards and upwards to bring us to that state where alone we become intimate with the real Master.

May your Love of the Form culminate in the Love of the Formless.

Maharaj Charan Singh

The role of the Master

The purpose of the physical form is achieved by explaining the teachings to you, putting you on the path and filling you with love and devotion for Shabd or Nam. Now we have to turn love and devotion for the physical form into love for Shabd or Nam, which ultimately is to pull us back to the Father.

Maharaj Charan Singh

Our spiritual maturity is reflected in our relationship with the Master. Many of us have reduced love to its physical expression, and consequently we believe that we need to be physically close to the physical Master to experience divine love. We may even believe that we should get directions from him concerning every aspect of our life. This is a misunderstanding of the role of the

Master. His role is not to get involved in solving the problems of our life. Those are to be addressed by us.

Sant Mat is meant for God-realization, for liberating the soul from its entanglement with the mind. The function of the Master is to be of help and guidance in achieving this goal. Baba Ji says his role is to inspire us to meditate, and he frequently guides us to start our journey by being natural to ourselves. If he is telling us to be natural, it is because our relationships with him, with the teachings and with life in general have become mechanical, superficial and artificial—all centred in the physical sphere. With such relationships as our yardstick, the results of any efforts are likely to be equally superficial. We behave in the way we think we ought to, based on concepts of what we believe spirituality and life to be, rather than starting with where and who we naturally are. Meditation gives us the means to develop a living relationship with the Master, with the teachings and with life, a relationship that will grow and flourish out of experience, that will mature with us and with our practice, and that is wholesome, natural and increasingly profound.

The Master wants us to go as deeply as possible into the nature of our path. He wants us to become spiritually grown up. Baba Ji says that if we are content to see just the physical form and we make no attempt to go within, then how will we ever know that the Master is not a fraud? How do we know that the Master is the embodiment of Shabd? Do we know? We may want to believe that he is, but we will not know it for a certainty until we first make the attempt and one day succeed in going inside, where alone we will know for ourselves.

To know Truth, we must seek the darshan of the Shabd form of the inner Master. Outer darshan should lead us to search inside, not stay content with the outside. Only by seeing the inner

Master will we know with certainty what difference there is, or
is not, between the physical form and the Radiant Form.

True darshan

A misconception that is frequently encountered on the path of
the Shabd Masters concerns darshan of the physical form of the
Master. People go to see the Master in the belief that through
his darshan their karmas will be cleared away. When we have
an opportunity to ask him a question in a meeting, we may prolong our question as much as possible, not because we want full
clarification, but because we calculate that by looking at the
physical form of the Master for as long as we can we are getting
our karmas washed away. This is just another deception of the
mind and we'd do well to wake up from such delusions.

Simply by looking at the Master, no karmas are cleared away.
That would be comparable to believing that just by going to see a
millionaire counting his money, we will also become millionaires.
It is his wealth, so how can we get it just by looking? Yet in the
case of the Master's darshan, we are assuming that by doing
exactly the same thing, that is, by looking at the Master, we
will get spiritually wealthy. The question is: Do we go to see the
Master to get something out of him or because we love him? In
love, there can be no bargaining, no calculations. If we are to keep
on the straight and narrow, we need to reflect regularly on our
motives and our way of understanding this supreme path of love.

Baba Ji says that when we are having darshan of the physical
form, if we are not gazing at the Master with absolute love, oblivi-
ous of everything else, then we are not having his darshan, we
are just looking. Darshan is the helplessness of the lover to look

at the beloved. It is not something that we can fake or force. It is a natural state born of love.

Darshan is complete absorption in the one we love. Receptiveness to the physical form can make it possible to have the darshan of the Radiant Form. And the way to become receptive to the Master's true nature is through meditation. Once this receptiveness is achieved, then the Master can grant the vision of his true form. It is up to him to give or not to give his vision: darshan cannot be taken, it is given by the Master. It is the prerogative of the Master to give when and where he wants, regardless of whether we are sitting right in front of him or anywhere from Auckland to Zanzibar.

> A thousand miles away is my Master's abode,
> But I always see him nearby.
> It's of little consequence if he's physically out of sight;
> My heart is his real home.
>
> Sultan Bahu

If we want to become intimate with our Master, we must meditate. Pretending that we can establish a true and eternal bond with the Master through visits to the Dera or by seeing him anywhere in the outside world is deluding ourselves, for the true relationship takes place on another plane altogether. A relationship created on the physical level without the support of meditation is a very shallow one. The way to achieve the true relationship is by making contact with the spiritual Master, and this can be done only through the practice of meditation—which can be done anywhere in the world.

We need to be clear that any spiritual progress that can be obtained at Dera can equally be obtained anywhere in the world.

The battleground is within us, wherever we are, and that is where the fight has to be fought. Our trouble is that it is a million times easier for us to travel thousands of miles to see the physical form of the Master than it is to bring our attention up one inch. Lack of spiritual courage and stamina makes us keep running to the outer form. The physical form of the Master is our starting place in understanding spirituality. It is also our safeguard in our battle with the deceits and deceptions of our mind. But the true intimacy with the true Master and real spiritual progress will only be obtained within us—through meditation. There is simply no other way. Every true Master says the same.

Your desire to visit India is welcome, but what I wish is that you may have no need for your physical hands, feet, and body, but travel without feet, speak without tongue, hear without ears, and see without eyes, and while sitting indoors visit not only India but the whole of Brahmand. If you saw India with the physical frame, what use, if you did not go beyond this world?

If you reply that you want to come to India for seeing your Guru, then it should be noted that the physical frame is not the real form of the Guru. It is a mere dress he has put on in this world and which will be put off here. The true form of the Guru is holy Sound, and in that form the Guru permeates every hair on your body and is seated within you. When you go above the eyes then the Guru will meet you in his radiant form, and when you reach Trikuti, the Guru will accompany you in his Sound Form, even up to Sach Khand.

Maharaj Sawan Singh

5

The practice of meditation

Be still, and know that I am God.

Psalms 46:10

The instant we sit for meditation is the moment we actually begin to tread the path of the saints. In that very moment all concepts are left behind and experience begins.

It is while we are sitting in meditation that we will come to the eye centre, make the mind motionless, go within, meet the Radiant Form, realize our deathless Self and achieve God-realization. All will happen while we are meditating. That is why it is said that meditating is action and meditating is enlightenment. Every time we sit in meditation we are doing the most important task a human being is capable of: that of completely transforming our character and consciousness.

Therefore, we should not believe our mind or society and feel guilty when they tell us: "Don't just sit there, do something." Rather, we should say: "Don't just do something, sit there!" The true value of meditation is kept hidden from others.

Sitting quietly, doing nothing, spring comes and the grass grows by itself.

Zen saying

91

It is by sitting for meditation that we empower our soul, receive spiritual nourishment, become spiritually strong to face the world and learn to make contact with the Shabd within. By sitting still we learn to surrender, to endure, to be patient and to accept the way of Shabd. By submitting to our Master's instructions to meditate, we nurture the seed of real humility, which is to live in his will. When we achieve a meditative state of mind, what can irritate us or shake our balance? In the midst of swirling activity, catastrophes or good fortune we remain unshakable, content and happy in our stillness at the eye centre. Such is the power of meditation. How can there be a more important activity in our day than sitting for meditation?

Preparation

There is no 'right way' to prepare for meditation, but there are many things we can do that will make our journey easier. Throughout the day we can prepare ourselves for meditation by doing simran whenever possible and by keeping the Master and the teachings in front of us in our various worldly activities. Then, our meditation practice will be the culmination of a whole day spent in a meditative atmosphere, and when we sit for our practice, it will be easier for us to concentrate at the eye centre.

To create a state of mind that is conducive to meditation, we can consciously try to abstain from anything that promotes anger, lust, tension and so forth. These things make strong impressions on the mind. We will discover that when we sit for meditation they will be the first things that will come to our mind and we will have to expend energy and time casting them out. Whenever possible, if these situations do arise, we can remember that our meditation will suffer if we indulge ourselves in them. Remembering this point, we should let them go.

Some people jump directly from bed to their meditation place. They take advantage of the sleepy state from which they find it easier to bring their attention to the eye centre. This is not always easily accomplished because the attention can drop to the throat centre and one again falls asleep. To prevent this from happening many choose to get their blood circulating by doing some form of exercise. Others prefer to splash water on their face or to take a shower. Still others prepare themselves by having a cup of tea or coffee. The important thing is that we are alert and fully awake. Then it will be easier to concentrate and we will be less likely to fall asleep.

To help prepare the mind for meditation some people like to read an inspirational book or article, or to begin meditation with a small prayer. As we all know, it takes time to settle the mind. The words our Master has given us for simran are the ideal tool to calm our mind, so we may dive right into our meditation. What better way to pray, to calm the mind and to instil an attitude of love and devotion than to use the words our Master has given us for that purpose?

As part of the preparation for our morning meditation, we can start the night before by having a light dinner and by going to bed early. When we go to bed, we can fall asleep doing our simran. In this way when we wake up we will find it easier to concentrate in meditation. Whatever we do to support our practice, Baba Ji advises us to be careful not to turn meditation into a ritual, into something that we do every day without even thinking why we do it. When preparing to get started in our meditation practice we can remember why it is that we meditate and what our goal is.

Time

Any time is a good time to start our meditation. If we wait for conditions to be ideal we might never sit for meditation. All times provide a good opportunity to calm and purify the mind, so we may do our meditation at any time of the day. For some people the best time to meditate is in the evening. At that time they feel more alert and, in order to get a relaxing sleep and to wake up invigorated and purified, they decide that evening meditation is best for them. Others are so tired at night that they are ready to sleep. For them the morning is the best time to meditate. At that time the mind is fresh and one is not burdened with responsibilities. In the early hours everybody is sleeping, the worries of the day have not yet started and there is no noise outside. For these reasons it may be easier to devote two and a half hours to meditation in the early morning because our worldly responsibilities make it hard for us to sit at some later time of the day. Nevertheless, some people prefer to meditate in the middle of the morning or afternoon.

In reality, the best time to meditate is the time *we* find best. We should evaluate the different aspects and responsibilities of our lives and then make our decision about which time is best for us, but we should try, if possible, to sit at the same time each day. If we decide to do our formal meditation practice in the morning, then we should try to give some additional time at night before we go to bed. If we choose to do our formal meditation at night, then we should try to give some additional time to sit in the morning as well. What better way to begin or end the day than by thanking the Master and letting go of all other agendas to be in touch with the source of peace and joy that is within ourselves?

To get full advantage of the atmosphere that is created by morning meditation, it is better that we do not go to sleep after

meditation. If, for instance, we begin our morning meditation at
3:00 a.m. and our daily activities begin at 8:00 a.m. and in the
gap between 5:30 and 8:00 in the morning we go to sleep, we
might consider beginning our meditation at 5:30 a.m. instead
of at 3:00 a.m. In this way there will be no gap between our
meditation practice and our daily routine, and we can derive
maximum benefit from the atmosphere created by our morning
meditation. But in this area there are no hard and fast rules
because meditation is good whether we sleep afterwards or
whether we don't. It is up to each one of us to see what works
best for us.

Place

If we don't have a special place to sit for meditation, we can try
to find a comfortable one that is conducive to our practice. Any
place will do. It will be helpful to sit in the same place, because
we will soon associate that place with the peace and tranquillity
of meditation, and we may find that our mind concentrates easier
when such an association is made. Although it is desirable that
the place is quiet and that we practise alone, sometimes our life
situation does not allow us to have privacy. If that is our case
and the only way we can meditate is by doing it in front of others,
then there is no harm in doing so. However, we should try to be
as inconspicuous as possible.

Posture

When sitting for meditation, it is important to sit in a relaxed
position with the spine and neck straight. The chin can be

slightly tucked in but not so much that it drops forward. Also, the head should not be tilted backwards or forwards. Both positions might induce us to fall asleep. The eyes should be closed and the attention held in the middle of the eyebrows at the spiritual eye centre. Be careful not to invert the eyes towards the eye centre. The hands can face upwards or downwards and can rest naturally on the knees or thighs. Our whole body should be at ease.

Meditation is an activity that involves both our mind and our body. If we don't adopt a posture that supports and helps the process of meditation, we will be obstructing our meditation practice. The important thing is to sit with our body motionless and our back upright and straight. This will help both our concentration and our health. It is not important whether we sit on a chair, Western style, or cross-legged on the floor, Indian style; both are fine ways to meditate. Many people are under the impression that sitting on a chair, Western style, is not as good as sitting cross-legged. This is a mistaken notion. Meditation is a matter of concentration. Some people spend years struggling to sit cross-legged, Indian style, and all the time that should have been devoted to concentration is spent with the attention on the legs, the pain or the cushions. The result is that such people spend less time in meditation than they would have if they had chosen to sit in a more comfortable position.

The mind cannot become calm and still if the body is constantly moving, just as water cannot be still in a glass that is moved. If we still the body we are helping to still our mind, so it is important to find a position in which we minimize the pain or discomfort that prompts us to shift uneasily every few minutes. If that means it is easier for us to sit on a sofa or a chair, then we can sit in that position, provided we sit upright and with the back straight. Not only is slouching detrimental for the back and more tiring after some time, it also prompts the mind to slouch, when it should be in an alert and poised state. It is not advised that we lie down because it is easier to fall asleep in such a position. We may experiment with different physical postures until we find the one that permits us to sit the maximum time without discomfort or falling asleep.

In no other position is the link between mind and body as clear as it is in our meditation posture. When we are depressed or lazy our back is hunched over and our head is hanging down. If we make the effort to sit upright, we shake off laziness and even pessimism. When we sit upright, it is difficult to have self-pity or to be negative. By assuming an upright posture, we inspire our mind to be awake and alert. If our posture and attitude are inspired, it becomes easier to concentrate and to enjoy our meditation. For bhajan (listening to the Shabd), we can sit in the squatting position, or cross-legged with the help of an arm support, or on a chair resting our elbows on a table or other arm support. The use of ear plugs is not advised by the Master.

Sometimes when we have been sitting for a period of time we feel a slight discomfort and want to move. We should continue to sit through this urge to move and discover how it is perfectly possible to resist the need to move or to scratch. Our mind has been trained to react immediately to anything that it dislikes. Expect the mind to fight and the body to become restless. The mind and the body are being trained to obey, and they don't like it. The body and the mind will not want to be confined, but we should keep holding the reins on them. After some time they will give in.

Baba Ji gives the following example to illustrate the importance of being still during meditation. He says that if we pick up a glass of water from a table and then place it back on the table, the water still continues to move even though the glass is not moving anymore. He calls this 'the ripple effect'. Likewise, if we move our body when we are meditating, even if it is a slight movement, that is enough to send ripples through the mind that disturb any calmness achieved. However, if we gently keep our mind on the words and do not move, soon we will experience how stilling the body helps to still and calm the mind, and, conversely, how stilling the mind helps to still the body. With the stillness of both body and mind, we begin to enjoy the peace that comes from concentration in meditation.

Concentration

Meditation means trying to hold our attention at the eye centre and not let it come down to the senses. That is concentration, to keep the mind steady at the eye centre and not let it come down.

Maharaj Charan Singh

Baba Ji says that the mind is like a computer: whatever we download into it, that is what we get. We input data of the physical world, and the mind collects impressions of material things. We input data of spirituality and the mind collects impressions of subtle things. The mind works equally well in both spheres. In meditation, we do not alter the nature of the mind, we simply input spiritual impressions and override worldly ones. In time, by the practice of concentrated meditation, the spiritual impressions will displace the worldly ones, replacing worldly desires by spiritual ones. In this way, the mind is automatically purified as it increasingly concentrates its attention inwards and upwards.

Concentration is similar to setting alight a piece of paper with a magnifying glass. A magnifying glass is held in such a way as to catch the sun's scattered rays and concentrate them onto a piece of paper. These little rays, when dispersed, are weak and harmless, but when collected together, held steady and focused through the magnifying glass, they become powerful enough to ignite the paper. One has to hold the glass very still, as any shaking will disturb the central point where the rays focus, and interrupt the process of generating heat sufficient to set the paper alight. When the glass has been held for some time a brilliant point appears on the paper, and if the point is held constant, it finally bursts into a flame.

In the same way, we are to collect every ray of our attention and focus it, without wavering, at the eye centre, until the intensity of our concentration in the simran kindles the Flame at the eye centre within. As we prolong our period of concentration, more and more of our attention gathers at the eye centre, and we become receptive to the inner Sound.

To understand what meditation is, we must understand the importance of concentration. Focused meditation will transform the way we perceive things and the way we live our life. Spiritual progress depends upon making the mind still at the eye centre, and concentration is what makes the mind still. Concentrated simran is the best way to train the mind to 'sit' at the eye centre. Our minds are used to jumping from one object to another, so to train the mind to concentrate on simran is a difficult task, but not an impossible one.

Concentrate on keeping your mind in the presence of the Lord; if it sometimes wanders and withdraws itself from Him, do not let it upset you; confusion serves rather to distract the mind than to recollect it; the will must bring it back calmly.

Brother Lawrence

We struggle in meditation because our attention is not concentrated in the simran, it is thinking about the world. From the moment we were born, the mind has come out of the eye focus and has been working outside. The outward tendency of the mind has become a very deep-rooted habit. We have to struggle to reverse this process if we are to concentrate our attention at the eye centre.

It is all a question of discipline, training and habit. Our concentration in meditation is in direct proportion to the degree to which we can detach ourselves from this world. We cannot pierce the darkness within because our attention has always been, and still is, caught up with our body, our attachments, neuroses and passions outside. Unless we develop detachment from everything outside and the capacity to concentrate within ourselves at the eye centre, we can make but little progress on the path. If we allow ourselves to indulge our physical nature, then, when we sit for meditation, our mind will get tossed about like a ship on a stormy sea and we will find we simply cannot concentrate. We then see for ourselves how an outward orientation scatters the attention, and how many of our actions and thoughts stand between us and concentration.

There is only one way to achieve concentration in meditation. We have to be ready to invert our outward and downward tendencies. We need to bring them inwards and upwards, through constant simran, to the eye centre, the seat of the soul.

The seat of the soul

> The third eye is the seat of the mind and soul. This is the pivotal point that holds the mystery of life. It is from here that our attention continually descends and spreads into the world through the nine outlets of the body ... From here every minute the mind wanders out. It does not sit still at this spot even for a moment. Its activities are legion. The ageless secret, the ancient wisdom, the path of the saints lies in drawing the attention back to this point.
>
> Maharaj Charan Singh

To invert the process by which our attention runs downwards into the world, the first thing we have to do is to locate the place in the vessel of our consciousness from where our attention leaks out. This place is what we know as the eye centre, the spiritual eye, the third eye or the seat of the soul. It is a common error to think of the eye focus as having some particular location in the brain or between or behind the eyes, measurable in terms of inches, centimetres or the points of the compass. We then try to locate this focus with our eyes or thoughts by attempting to place the attention physically between the eyebrows.

When we approach meditation like this, we are very far away from the eye focus. The mind is jumping around, groping blindly for something or somewhere. It is running out by trying to think about the focus, instead of simply relaxing and being in the darkness with the eyes closed. The process of thinking indicates that the mind is scattered, while concentration at the eye focus means the absence of even the slightest twitching of thought. If we are thinking of the eye centre, it means we cannot be in it. If we are in the centre, we will not be thinking of it.

> When you close your eyes, you are there where you should be. Being there, do simran, concentrate. When you close your eyes, you are nowhere outside. You are just here at the eye centre.
>
> Maharaj Charan Singh

Throughout this book we have seen how, over and over again, all Masters emphasize the paramount importance of bringing and keeping the attention within ourselves, at the seat of the soul. In the following letter from *Spiritual Gems*, Master Sawan Singh explains how to do it:

> Answering your question as to the best way to reach and hold the focus, I can only repeat the substance of what you already have been given ...
>
> That method is the same as all Saints use, which is simply the concentrated attention held firmly at the given centre. What else can we say? It is all a matter of unwavering attention. Every ray of attention must be centred there and held there. If one strays away for a time, one has lost the advantage. It may be said safely that if any earnest student should hold his attention fully upon the given centre for three hours, without wavering, he must go inside. But that is not so easy without long practice. However, by and by, the mind becomes accustomed to staying in the centre. It rebels

less and less, and finally yields to the demand to hold to the centre. Then your victory is won.

Before that, the mind will not remain still for a long time. It jumps around like a monkey. But after a time it will give in and settle down. It is a matter of will to hold to the centre, also not to forget nor allow the attention to go off after some other thought or experiences. One easily forgets and then the mind drops down. A keenly awakened intelligence must hold to the centre, steadily, every moment. If any thought enters the consciousness, jerk the mind back to the centre and hold it there. Make the spirit, instead of the mind, the commander of the situation. The mind is tricky and will run out if permitted. Conquer it. But to conquer it is not easy, of course, and it takes time.

The problem is not complicated at all. The whole thing is just attention, and then unbroken attention, at the eye centre, allowing no other thought to intrude itself into the consciousness and lead you away from the centre. This was the method by which I won my way inside and it is the method by which you must win your way. It is the old method of all Saints.

The reason you nearly reach it, as you say, and then lose it, is because you cannot hold the mind still. It is somewhat like a wild animal which has been accustomed to run about in the forest. When captured, it is in great distress if held still in the hands of the captor. But like that animal, by and by it will yield and obey if we persist in our efforts. The repetition of the Names is to help in holding the mind at the eye centre. That is the value of the Names ...

We must enter it if we persist. All the powers of the spirit, the real *atma* [soul] in man, gather at the focus by means of this concentrated thought; and then, by means of

accumulated force (through bhajan and simran), we break
through the curtain and enter the light.

Maharaj Sawan Singh

From concepts to experience

Unless we withdraw our attention to the eye centre, we cannot concentrate within and take even the first step of our
spiritual journey Homeward.

Maharaj Charan Singh

The Masters couldn't be clearer that reaching the eye centre is
the first goal on the way to achieve a higher degree of spirituality.
Yet in spite of this, some will feel that now they have been initiated, they should concern themselves with nothing short of God-
realization. Although our ultimate goal is clearly God-realization,
to overlook the crucial steps that take us there is counterproductive
and may be used as a trick against us by our clever mind. We do
not yet possess absolute love, and without this ingredient we cannot merge back in Shabd and attain God-realization. Pure love
is to lose our own identity and to become another being. As long
as we continue to function with a strong sense of a separate self,
it will be utterly impossible for us to achieve union with Shabd.
God-realization, therefore, is out of the question at the stage
where we are at present, so to invest in God-realization at this
stage is impractical, fruitless and unrealistic.

   If, for the moment, our immediate goal is not to be God-
realization, then should we not be aiming at least for Self-realization? There is no doubt that before we can achieve God-
realization we must first attain realization of our own true nature.

But Self-realization is a very high stage in which the soul realizes what it is and cries out: "I am That, I am the Deathless Self" (Sohang). Our minds are still immersed in duality and we do not yet have the purity required to experience such a degree of realization. For the moment, then, we have to put aside the goal of Self-realzation, just as we saw the wisdom of putting aside an immediate goal of God-realization.

Before we can realize what we are, we need to have contacted the spiritual form of the Master. But if we have not yet passed through the inner stars, sun and moon, we cannot have seen the Radiant Form. If that is the case, then our immediate goal should be to cross the planes that stand between us and his Radiant Form. In order to cross those planes, we need first to have pierced the barrier of the physical by dying while living— by experiencing a near-death experience while sitting consciously in meditation. This, like the glass that magnifies the sun's rays, will happen when we collect and focus all our attention at the eye centre, and we pass to the astral plane.

So if we haven't broken the barrier of the physical by passing through the eye centre, our first task has to be to make the mind motionless by collecting our scattered attention at the eye focus. And there, finally, we have our immediate and primary goal. The eye centre! For most of us, the eye centre is our spiritual goal and our purpose in life. To reach the eye centre and to keep our attention concentrated there is a realistic and do-able goal. The eye centre is the place we will start our journey. It has to be the only goal that concerns us. It alone provides the means by which we will gain spiritual transport.

Reaching the eye centre will give us the spiritual experience that will support an unwavering faith in the Master and the teachings. The fact that it is a more humble goal than the ultimate goal of God-realization doesn't make it less necessary or any easier. To achieve it we will need to concentrate all our attention, love, devotion, energy, intelligence, skill and effort on the task. To reduce and still our thought waves by means of simran at the eye centre—this has to become our main concern and challenge in life.

> The first step, then, is to withdraw our consciousness to the eye centre.
>
> Maharaj Charan Singh

On going inside the eye centre, we will realize that in truth we are spiritual beings, whereas without this realization, the statement that we are spiritual beings will remain forever just one more mental concept with which we decorate our mental shelves. Without first reaching the eye centre, no spiritual progress can be made. It is prudent, therefore, that before God-realization, Self-realization, the Radiant Form or the inner planes, and given the scale of the transformation we have to achieve, we make the eye centre our immediate and unmitigated goal.

> So long as we remain away from this point and do not catch hold of the Sound Current, salvation remains a distant dream.
>
> Maharaj Charan Singh

The rewards are unimaginable and the treasure is waiting for us:

> Your wildest dreams or imaginings cannot picture the grandeur of what lies within. But the treasure is yours and is there for you. You can have it whenever you go there. Take

it from me, and once and for all, that everything, including
the Creator, is within you, and whosoever has attained it,
has attained it by going inside the eye focus.

Maharaj Sawan Singh

Simran

It is possible to pray at all times, in all circumstances and in
every place, and easily to rise from frequent vocal prayer to
prayer of the mind and from that to prayer of the heart,
which opens up the Kingdom of God within us.

Saint John Chrysostom

Baba Ji says that when we sit for meditation, we should be
absolutely relaxed, start our simran and let ourselves go. Therefore, the first step in meditation is to place simran at the eye
centre. It takes a deliberate act to extract our mind from its
involvement with its thoughts. We have to take our mind away
from its thinking and consciously contain it in simran. At the
beginning of meditation, simran feels like taming a wild animal.
That is why it is helpful to acknowledge that we are letting go of
our involvement with the world, and say to ourselves, "Now I
am letting go of my thoughts and I am placing my mind in
simran." By doing this, we begin to gather our attention together.
From being spread out in every direction, we begin to draw it
towards a focus that can contain it. This is a good way to start
our meditation session.

If we begin in an unfocused way, our meditation continues
to be unfocused throughout. Soon we are so involved with our
thoughts that we are thinking instead of meditating. We are then

indulging in thinking, fuelling desires, trying to make real our world of make-believe. When we recognize that we are thinking and we release those thoughts, we are remembering the teachings and challenging our mental laziness. Each time we let go of our thoughts and go back to our simran, we win a heroic and courageous victory. We are, as it were, swimming against the current, returning home to our source. We are inverting the downward tendencies of the mind; we are turning our attention upwards, to the eye centre.

Baba Ji says that doing simran is, for the soul, like untying a balloon from the string that holds it. Once the balloon is untied, it naturally starts to rise up. We cannot force our consciousness to go up. The consciousness will go up on its own as a natural result of being freed from its absorption with the world—through doing our simran.

> Please make no attempt to take the soul up by force. The soul will find its own way.
>
> Maharaj Sawan Singh

By switching our thoughts to simran, we extract ourselves from the world of concepts. We let go of the need to be endlessly entertained by our thoughts, give up our addiction to inner chattering and step out onto the path of inner peace. Our practice of simran is the time to train our minds to be still at the eye centre. If during our meditation practice we are not alert, vigilant and sharp in recognizing and releasing thoughts, we are not meditating but indulging ourselves. Thinking is not meditation. Those thoughts will gain momentum, they will become strong, and soon our meditation will be over. Instead of moving into a peaceful yet alert state of mind, we will continue living in a world of concepts, indulging the very same fantasies that till now have prevented us from knowing what it is to be fully awake and fully alive.

If, by contrast, we make an effort to keep our mind in simran, to gather our attention at the eye focus, then the soul gradually regains its power. The stronger and more effective our practice, the weaker our world of concepts will become. The stronger we become, the more real, potent and transforming our meditation practice becomes.

There is beauty in simran—in just doing it. Concentrating in simran produces a beautiful, simple joy. Once we learn to concentrate on the words, the question of boredom doesn't arise. We don't have to ask the Master for results. Simran is the practice and becomes in and of itself the reward. We become bored when mentally we don't want to be where we are; when we want to skip the effort and jump to astral travelling and seeing things inside, when we ignore the opportunity to derive peace from the effort itself. We must first learn to settle the mind in simran, and stay there, enjoying the practice with gratefulness and humility. That in itself is a spiritual accomplishment. If we are able to keep the mind in simran throughout the day, we will experience its benefits within ourselves; meditation then becomes the crowning glory of a prize already in hand.

There is no mode of life in the world more pleasing and more full of delight than continual conversation with God; only those who practise and experience it can understand it.

Brother Lawrence

By the practice of placing our simran at the eye focus, we achieve peace of mind and taste for ourselves a gladness of heart that has nothing to do with external events. We develop confidence in the reasons why we meditate. We do it with enthusiasm because we know it brings us peace. We see for ourselves the futility of indulging in thinking and of fuelling outside problems, concerns and emotions. We are willing to give up those fantasies because we have experienced the benefits of doing so.

Simran then becomes a practical, reasonable and sensible way to live. By its practice, we move along our journey from the world of concepts to that of spiritual experience. Adopting spirituality as the most desirable way of life, we discover that the clarity of mind that comes with the practice of simran makes us more skilful in everything we do. Concentrating in simran, our meditation feels good. We enjoy the ride because we have learnt to let go—we have already experienced where our thoughts would take us and we don't want to go there. We take a holiday from the tyranny of our own nagging chitchat—we relish peace because we have tranquillized our mind in simran, at the eye centre.

One who accustoms himself to this appeal [of continuous interior prayer] experiences as a result so deep a consolation and so great a need to offer the prayer always, that he can no longer live without it.

The Way of a Pilgrim

The stability we achieve with simran doesn't happen by a miracle. We achieve it through effort and by applying ourselves to the instructions to do simran over and over again. Once we can take rest in our own simran, we begin to feel that the wild beast of the mind is now being tamed. We are leaving the confusing world of concepts; we have the satisfaction that we are applying our knowledge of the teachings practically. We start to awaken from our deep sleep of worldly indolence. Light is dawning on the long dark night of our soul.

No one can describe the glory of the moment when the mind is still and the soul is in a state of complete absorption.

Soami Ji Maharaj

Simran will not come automatically in the beginning, so we have to make an effort to establish the habit. With constant effort, little by little we see that our practice of simran changes into effortless effort, just like driving and other tasks that take time and practice to accomplish but, once established, we do in an effortless manner.

No one should give the answer that it is impossible for a man occupied with worldly cares ... to pray always. Everywhere, wherever you may find yourself, you can set up an altar to God in your mind by means of prayer. And so it is fitting to pray at your trade, on a journey, standing at the counter or sitting at your handicraft ... By the power of the invocation of the Name of God ... [one] would come to know from experience that frequency of prayer, this sole means of salvation, is a possibility for the will of man.

Saint John Chrysostom

To strengthen our simran practice, it is helpful to associate the words of our simran with the Master. These are the very words that the Master gave us at initiation, and our association with the Master and these words is, in fact, inseparable. When somebody mentions the name of someone we love, the image of that person comes to mind. In the same way, repetition of simran can be our cue to be mindful of our Master. If we then associate particular routine activities in our daily life with doing simran, we gradually help our mind become aware of the Master's presence throughout the day.

> Persons who repeat the holy names of God
> Have angels around them.
>
> Hazrat Muhammad

We can start by choosing one action that we do every day and decide to be entirely in the simran while doing that action, without any mental commentary. When practised in this way, we find that simran helps us to live in the moment and get more out of life. When we walk, we can try to associate walking with simran. Before we eat or drink, we can take a moment to acknowledge the Master's presence and give thanks with our simran. This can be done with our eyes open. We don't need to advertise our spirituality. When we are waiting in an office or a queue, we can practise our simran. During work, we can take a few moments to acknowledge his presence—even if it's only for a second or two. Cooking, gardening and doing other manual labour offer excellent opportunities to get immersed in simran.

Simran can continue whether we are showering, dressing, making up a bed, opening a door or switching the computer on. We can turn all these activities into opportunities to trigger the remembrance of our Master by associating these activities regularly with simran. Whatever it is that we are doing, we can decide to be entirely in simran for that particular action. After some time, we can move to another action and then to another one, until most of our day our attention is kept in simran. This way we will become present to our life. We don't walk a step ahead of ourselves, or a step behind, but fully present and living in the moment. After all, our life is made up of a continuous string of moments. Being present to each will improve the quality of our life and will strengthen us in living the spiritual way.

> I keep myself in His presence by simple attentiveness and a loving gaze upon God, which I can call the actual presence of God or, to put it more clearly, an habitual, silent and secret conversation of the soul with God; which sometimes causes me interior, and often exterior, happiness and joy.
>
> Brother Lawrence

Simran must be done mentally, and nobody outside should be able to hear what we are repeating. It is all a matter of creating the habit. Unceasing simran is the secret door to a life that is filled with devotion.

> You do not need to speak out loud
> For he is the Knower
> Of all that is secret,
> Of all that is hidden:
> God – no God but He! –
> To Him belong
> The most beautiful names.
>
> Qur'an

Constant simran will lead us to feel the divine in our life. This itself then becomes our practice. Loving repetition of the names will naturally make us aware of the constant presence of the Master. To be successful in this practice, the repetition of the words should be done at a comfortable pace: not so fast that we get anxious, nor so slow that we fill the gaps in between the words with thoughts. We will feel the Master's presence like a warm comfort inside and around us. Our Master's presence in our daily activities will change our relationship with him. He will cease being the Master who is far away from us in Dera and instead become our everyday companion and intimate friend. He will be the close friend who shares our laughter and sorrows, our joys and pains, our difficulties and successes. Through the deepening of our formal meditation practice, and through the habit of remembering him in our daily activities, our understanding of the path will grow stronger and we will know without doubt that he has always been with us. He is with us now, and he will always be with us. Paraphrasing Farid, one could say:

> Sugar, buffalo milk and chocolates, all are sweet,
> But incomparably sweeter
> Is the repetition of the names of my Lord,
> Like pure warm honey melting in my heart.

Dhyan

> O Beloved! I have heard many a tale
> About your wondrous beauty;
> But now that I have beheld you within,
> I see that you are really
> A thousand times more wonderful
> Than the tales depict you.
>
> Hafiz

When the Master initiated us, he made it clear that the Radiant Form is always with us. This is not wishful thinking or a figment of our imagination, it is something that can be known once we have worked within ourselves to realize this truth. Layers upon layers of fears, attachments, passions, desires, cravings and illusions cover our inner eye and prevent us from realizing that this is so. Baba Ji says that seeing the Radiant Form is the natural result of concentrated simran. True dhyan is effortless; it is the grace of the Master.

Simran brings our attention to the eye centre and dhyan helps us to keep it there. If we are swimming in a river against the current, we need to grasp on to a rock to rest ourselves, so we have the strength to continue swimming against the current to our destination. In like manner, simran helps us to swim against the downward tendencies of the mind and dhyan is the rock that allows us to rest so that we can make further progress.

Even if we close our eyes and see only darkness, this can be an inner experience in itself that will begin to awaken the dhyan or 'seeing faculty' of the soul. In that darkness is where our meditation begins. As soon as our attention is fully in that darkness, we are at the threshold of the door to our home. This is the doorway to eternity. From then on, it is just a question of holding our attention in the darkness with simran, of developing progressively deeper concentration, until we are so absorbed in inner perception that we don't feel our body at all. We will then experience, instead, a new level of awareness.

In dhyan, it is the attention that does the 'seeing'. There is no need to focus on the eye centre with the eyes or to try to invert them inwards. The physical eyes have nothing whatsoever to do with the seeing faculty of the soul, just as the ears have nothing to do with the hearing faculty of the soul. In both cases, it is concentrated attention that awakens both faculties. Great Master says:

> When your concentration is almost complete, then, in place of darkness in the eye centre, sparks and fleeting flashes of light will begin to appear, and then light will be steady and the soul automatically will leave the body and enter the *tisra til* [third eye].

The dark sky that we are aware of immediately upon closing our eyes is like a screen in a movie theatre. It is the very same sky in which the inner stars, sun, moon and Radiant Form will make their appearance when concentration deepens. So, there is great significance in that darkness and we shouldn't be afraid of it; rather, it should be appreciated and loved. When we have gained more concentration in simran, the seeing faculty will naturally develop and the darkness will be replaced by light within.

> On a dark night,
> Inflamed by love and longing,
> (O exquisite adventure!)
> Undetected I slipped away,
> My house, at last, grown still.
> Secure in the darkness,
> I climbed the secret ladder in disguise,
> With no other light or guide
> Than the one burning in my heart.
> This light led the way
> More clearly than the rising sun,

To where he was waiting for me,
The one I knew so intimately,
In a place where no one could find us.
O night that guided me!
O night sweeter than sunrise!
O night that joined lover with Beloved,
Lover transformed in Beloved!

Saint John of the Cross

Bhajan

Bhajan simply means attending to the Sound Current,
which is also termed by the saints as the practice of Shabd
Yoga. This is done by the soul, or by its attention. It is
through surat or soul that the divine melody is heard. The
practice awakens the soul that has been slumbering for ages
and results in a state of bliss.

Maharaj Sawan Singh

Bhajan is the act of being receptive to the resonating power of
Shabd. If we don't hear anything, we should keep our attention
on the silence, and be present in our longing to hear the Sound.
With practice, the hearing faculty of the soul will be awakened
and we will hear the Sound. Regardless of whether we hear anything or not, we must always sit for bhajan. Sound is always
there, but we need to train the mind to be receptive to it. We
need to acquire the habit of sitting for bhajan. This is the way
we will become receptive to the subtlety of the Sound and nurture love for it.

Your attention may remain focused for no more than a minute or two, or five or ten, or it may barely hear the Sound, but even then the news of your effort will reach right into Sach Khand, that you are offering a prayer.

Baba Jaimal Singh

The reason we don't hear the Shabd is because our soul is covered with layers of karmas and is consequently unable to make contact with the divine. The practice of meditation removes these coverings. Only the Shabd-dhun, the vibratory sound of the Shabd, with its power to purify all that come in contact with it, can dissolve these karmas. It is by being in touch with the Shabd that we become free so that we can return to our true home.

When you sit in bhajan, begin by attaching the mind and attention to the sound that you hear first—which is like that of a grain handmill, or a steam locomotive, or an oven going full blast—and keep the faculty of inner seeing and hearing directed upward to focus on where the sound is coming from. Then attach the mind and attention to the sound of the bell, and next to that of the conch. The soul will then gently savour the bliss, and one day it will surely reach Sach Khand. Please do not be in a hurry. When the soul becomes steadfast in its love for the Sound, a bond is then forged with the Shabd-dhun. Thus step by step, slowly, slowly, the mind is tamed. One day you will certainly reach Sach Khand.

Baba Jaimal Singh

Many of us only do simran and do not sit for bhajan. We must remember that simran, even if it has become sweet and satisfying, is nothing compared to contact with the divine melody within. Simran is only a means; the real spiritual practice is being receptive to the Shabd. Simran is like preparing food. Bhajan is like eating it. Who would go through all the trouble of preparing food to eat and then, when the food is ready, not eat it? And yet that is precisely what we are doing when we sit for meditation and attend only to our simran and neglect to do our bhajan.

Each time we sit, even if it is only for fifteen minutes, we should create the habit of becoming receptive to the Shabd-dhun by giving some time to bhajan. Even if we don't hear a thing, we should develop the habit of being receptive to whatever is there. Even if what we hear is silence, we should pay attention to it. That silence will give rest to our mind, will settle the thought waves, and from that silence, the Sound, Shabd-dhun, will become audible. If we don't practise being receptive, how will we ever listen to the Shabd? If we don't become receptive, how will we ever obtain the full benefit of our meditation?

This is why it is important that in each sitting we must give time first to simran, and then to bhajan. When the prescribed time for bhajan arrives, we should switch from the simran position to the bhajan position, regardless of whether we achieved or didn't achieve any concentration during the simran session.

The light and sound of Shabd are already within us. We might imagine covering a speaker or a bright light with many layers of cloth. In such a situation, we would not be able to hear the sound nor see the light, nor even be aware of their existence. However, once we begin removing the coverings, we will first hear or see a faint glimmer of sound or light. As we remove each covering, the sound and light will grow in intensity. Finally, if we can remove all the coverings, we will make contact with the source of the sound and light. Similarly, through meditation we remove the layers of karma from our soul and experience this sound and light, which are already present.

A bamboo flute makes sound because it is hollow and empty within. It is impossible to make any sound with a pipe that is filled, let alone play a tune. To give up our thoughts during meditation is to become an empty bamboo flute. In emptiness of self we become receptive to the divine melody that is constantly reverberating in every cell of our body. We then experience with full force the music of the Shabd within ourselves. The Shabd Masters tell us that nothing compares to living life consciously in the Sound Current.

> Devotion to the Shabd consists in turning inward and listening one-pointedly to its melody. The Sound is subtle, and unless we ourselves become subtle, we cannot hear it ... This Sound is resounding all the time. Why then do we not hear it? The reason is that waves are constantly arising in our minds and we are full of selfhood and pride.
>
> Maharaj Sawan Singh

Inner experiences

> The soul has penetrated into the peak, O friend,
> And pierced, like a shaft, a hole in the sky.
> Therein she beheld sights wondrous,
> Beyond comprehension.
> Even as the cannonball blasts the gate of a citadel,
> So did the soul burst the tower gate of the fortress.
> She got linked to the Lord as pearls to a thread.
> She went zooming through the lane of the firmament,
> O friend, with joy and bliss filling her heart.

She was bestowed the boon of realizing Him, O Tulsi,
In a realm without trees, seeds or creation.

Tulsi Sahib

During meditation we might experience inner visions. However, the object of meditation is not to enjoy inner visions but to transcend them. Usually the inner visions we have are impressions that the mind has accumulated over many lifetimes. If we pay attention to them or get absorbed by them they will keep us from our goal.

We must hold our attention at the eye centre, keep on doing our simran, or listening to the Sound, and slowly all these images will fade away and vanish. If we experience spiritual transport, we must always keep our attention fixed at the eye centre in simran, dhyan of the Master or hearing the inner Sound. Just as when we watch a film, we simply go on watching, fully knowing that it is only a movie, with nothing real about it, in the same manner we must remain indifferent to all that comes and goes before us on the inner planes until we reach the Master's Radiant Form. From then on, the Radiant Form is there to give us directions and to lead us by the hand.

> You are not imagining things, and in the course of time you
> will yourself feel and know that what you see inside is more
> real than that which you see outside.

Maharaj Charan Singh

If we have an inner experience, it is best not to get attached to it or to try to reproduce it when we sit again in meditation. We should only be concerned about keeping our attention on the words or the Sound. Whether inner experiences come or they don't come, we shouldn't be concerned. If we do our meditation practice with any other attitude, we run the risk of doing it with expectations, and if the results we expect do not come, we become frustrated. Then, after a while we might even stop meditating. That is one of the reasons why it is important to attach ourselves to the effort and leave the results in his hands.

We should not talk about our inner experiences to others regardless of how close the relationship. If we vomit the food we are given, how will we get spiritual nourishment? Talking of inner experiences is likely to distort them, and we run the risk of inflaming our egos, with the result that we lose the benefits of whatever progress we have made. By remaining silent and digesting our inner experience within, we will continue our progress on the inner path.

Conclusion

Brave is he who has control over his mind and senses,
for the inward progress is in proportion to this con-
trol. It is the repetition that brings the mind in, and
the Sound Current that pulls it up. Inside us there
are inexhaustible treasures. There the Lord himself is
with us. Only he who has gone within can appreciate
this; others have no idea of it.

Maharaj Sawan Singh

Indulging in thinking prevents us from concentrating our attention at the eye centre and becoming one with Shabd. Ego feeds
on this disease and becomes stronger by it. Ego has overtaken
our soul like a cancer and wreaks havoc on every aspect of our
life. We are spiritually sick, and meditation is the only medication that will cure us. If we don't take our medication, how can
we regain our health?

We keep on talking, reading and discussing the path. Enough
has been said. Enough has been written. We can go on talking
and reading for the rest of our lives, but talk is cheap and more
books will not give us the experience of the saints. Once we have
been initiated, we don't need more books, more discussions,
more recordings or more running after the physical form of the
Master. We don't need more concepts. What we need is experi-

ence—less information; more transformation. To achieve that vital transformation, the only thing we need to concern ourselves with is our medication—doing our simran as much as we can throughout the day and sitting for meditation every day. If we truly and sincerely practise the method of the Shabd Masters, we will become better human beings, we will experience knowledge of the deathless Self, and we will realize the divine.

The whole purpose of every satsang, of every Sant Mat book and of the Master working so hard for us day in and day out is to give us one simple message: You can do your meditation. You can concentrate better in meditation. You have the strength to do it. Just do it. It's time to put away the books. Sit down for action and awaken to the Shabd.

The ultimate book on meditation is *Die to Live*. In closing, let us remember in the loving words of its author, Shabd Master Charan Singh, the importance of doing meditation:

I can tell you one thing: just attend to your meditation. There's no other way, there's no other short cut. By attending to meditation you are automatically progressing towards your destination, and you will become another being and lose your identity. Meditation is the only remedy. There's no other way to lose your identity. When there is so much rust on a knife, the only way to remove it is to rub the knife against the sandstone. Otherwise, the rust won't go, the knife won't shine. Mere talk won't solve your problem; intellectual discussion won't lead you anywhere. The main thing is practice.

The Lord gives us hunger; the more we attend to meditation, the more hungry we become. When we become hungry, He provides us with food. As Christ said, the harvest is ready. The harvest is always ready, but we have to lift our consciousness to that level where we can collect that harvest.... Just change your way of life according to the teachings and attend to meditation. That is all that is required. From meditation, love will come, submission will come, humility will come. Everything will come.

for further reflection

This world is perishable and so are all worldly things. The wise man is he who realizes the transitory and illusory nature of this world and all things pertaining to it, and makes the best use of this body by worshipping the Supreme Being, through bhajan and simran. He thus derives benefit from all that the Creator, through His grace, has placed in the body, and takes that priceless jewel, the essence of all—the surat (the soul)—to its real abode.

Soami Ji Maharaj

To subjugate the mind, the technique is: first, to receive the Satguru's instructions; second, to hear the Shabd-dhun; third, to love the Dhun; and fourth, to experience its bliss. Only then does the Satguru's form settle in the mind. The form of the Satguru's face will then be seen in the mind as clearly as we see our own face in a mirror. When day by day the mind's faculty of focused attention, which is an aspect of the soul, becomes pure through continuous practice, and all worldly desires have left the mind, the mind will never follow any external attractions, but stay only with the Satguru's form. Then the Satguru will look upon the disciple with his glance of mercy; and as the Satguru's compassionate glance keeps falling upon the disciple, all the gross and evil tendencies of the mind will go away, and the mind will love the soul. The flow of consciousness will then love the Shabd's current, and the celestial sound, taking measure of that soul's worth, will blend it within itself, giving it a little taste of the spiritual bliss.

Baba Jaimal Singh

An ounce of practice is better than a ton of knowledge. What use is it to know the principles if one does not live them. A learned person without practice is no better than a beast of burden carrying a load of books on its back. It is infinitely better to practise than to preach. Example is better than precept.

Maharaj Jagat Singh

I am surprised at the people of this world!
How is it that they never think of their own welfare?
They seem so sure of themselves,
But who will help them on their last day?
Why are they so carefree?
What answer will they give to the messenger of death?
Have they forgotten that they will die?
What are they so pleased about?
What is wrong with them?
Is there anything they cannot do?
Why don't they remember the Lord
And be free from bondage?
It will cost them nothing!

Tukaram

In the beginning, we have to make an effort to renounce ourselves, but after that there is no longer anything but unutterable contentment. When we face difficulties, we have only to run back to the Lord and ask Him for His grace. When He grants it, everything becomes easy.

It is a common thing to just be content to do penances and private spiritual exercises, forgetting about love which is the end and purpose of it all. It is easy to recognize this by the works that such things produce and that is why so little concrete spiritual virtue can be found.

It is not necessary to have either a keen intellect or great knowledge to go to God, but simply a heart resolved to apply itself to Him and for Him, and to love only Him.

Brother Lawrence

There's no set prayer which you can repeat four times a day or five times a day. No language is required, no words are required in prayer. Prayer is a language of love from the heart of the Father, and nobody exists then between you and the Father. You're not conscious of the world when you pray to Him. He exists and you exist. That is real prayer, and that is only possible at the time of meditation when we try to forget all that we are and where we are.

Maharaj Charan Singh

The light on your face,
you will take with you.
All else, your sorrows, your joys
and all that you lay claim on,
you will leave behind.
The light on your face,
that you will take.

Shaikh Abu-Saeed

The minute I heard my first love story
I started looking for you, not knowing
how blind that was.

Lovers don't finally meet somewhere.
They're in each other all along.

Rumi

Endnotes

Note: Classic texts are referenced by standard citations wherever possible (page, section and/or verse numbers). At times the language of the translations of these classics has been modernized. When the translation of a quotation from a classic has been based on a particular source, the book is given in the bibliography and the translation is noted as "See [source on which translation is based]".

Dedication Page
Whether the answer to your question... *Die to Live*, 274:359. Because some readers may not be familiar with the term 'bhajan and simran', which Master Charan Singh used in the original quotation, 'bhajan and simran' has been translated as 'meditation' for this dedication. For definitions of 'bhajan' and 'simran' see Chapter 1.

Introduction
1   **As long as you do not die while living...** Quoted in *Die to Live*, 30.
2   **I know those habits that can ruin your life...** *I Heard God Laughing: Renderings of Hafiz*, 15.
3   **Constantly mastering his mind...** *Bhagavad Gita*, VI:15.
4   **The beginning and end of all things...** *Philosophy of the Masters*, vol. 4, 120.
5   **There is a difference between knowing...** *The Matrix*, Warner Brothers Pictures, Los Angeles, 1999. Retrieved 30 October, 2003 from http://www.matrixunplugged.net/matrix.php?page=quotes.
8   **All rivers merge in the Ocean...** Indian saying.

Chapter 1: Spiritual beings going through a human experience

9   **This life is but a link...** *The Science of the Soul*, 194:29.

9   **we are spiritual beings...** Often attributed to Pierre Teilhard de Chardin, but research indicates this is not in his writings.

10   **Indian word 'Kal'...** Kal is the divine or supernatural power that includes both the God of this world and the devil in the same being, a concept that is difficult to grasp for many in the West, as there is little precedent for it in Western tradition. However, a few such references do exist. For instance, we can find the following verse in the Bible: "I form the light and create darkness: I make peace and create evil: I the Lord do all these things." (Bible, *Isaiah*, 45:7) In the spiritual Masters' order of creation, Kal is this creation's administrator, arbitrator and officiator, servant of the One, who is the Creator beyond the reach of time. Kal is both the individual mind and the universal mind, the downward tendencies of the mind as well as the mind's upward tendencies.

10   **In his Radiant Form...** *Die to Live*, 23.

11   **Look upon the world as a bubble...** *The Dhammapada*, 54–55:170–171.

11   **we are so attached to the creation...** Noted by Charan Singh in *Spiritual Discourses*, vol. 2, 40.

12   **Everyone is burning in the fire...** *Spiritual Letters*, 80:4.

13   **In a place where mind and matter...** *Spiritual Gems*, 233:148.

13   **Pleasures from external objects...** *Bhagavad Gita*, V:22.

13   **Liberty means responsibility...** "Liberty". Cited in *Oxford Dictionary of Quotations*, 497.

15   **Develop the power to withdraw...** *Spiritual Gems*, 120–121:89. Italics added by Esponda.

15   **The power within is not ignorant...** *Spiritual Gems*, 73:47.

16   **One does not become a satsangi...** *The Science of the Soul*, 181:1.

17   **Mind is the deadliest of foes...** *Die to Live*, 11.

18   **Intellect is a great barrier in our way...** *Die to Live*, 60:27.

18   **Relentlessly and restlessly, the mind...** *Die to Live*, 11.

20   **While the mind derives its life-force...** *Discourses on Sant Mat*, 274.

21   **Satsangis should form the habit...** *The Science of the Soul*, 189:18.

23   **If the doors of perception were cleansed...** "A Memora-
ble Fancy", pl.14. Cited in *Oxford Dictionary of Quotations*, 88.

24   **Open your eyes...** *Epictetus: the Art of Living: a New Interpretation by Sharon Lebell*, 7.

25   **Happiness and freedom begin with...** *Epictetus: the Art of
Living: a New Interpretation by Sharon Lebell*, 3.

30   **Within the body He Himself resides...** Adi Granth, 754.

31   **What has happened...** *Kulliyat Bulleh Shah*, 270:124, translated in *Bulleh Shah: The Love-Intoxicated Iconoclast*.

32   **union is achieved...** See *How to Know God: The Yoga Aphorisms of Patanjali*, 11.

33   **One day I wiped out all notions...** *The Little Zen Companion*,
187.

33   **When the desire for the Friend...** *Nobody, Son of Nobody*,
39:210.

Chapter 2: Priorities, attitude and effort

35   **Seek ye first the kingdom of God...** Bible, *Matthew* 6:21.

35   **a servant who is sent by a king...** Based on an account by
Rumi. See *Discourses of Rumi*, 26.

38   **To know that enough is enough...** See *Tao Te Ching*,
XLVI:105.

38   **Do not waste time uselessly...** *Spiritual Letters*, 168:111.

39   **This constant feeling of loneliness...** *Quest for Light*, 6:10.

39   **All the misfortunes of men...** *The Translation of Pensées*, tr.
L. Brunschvicg, 5th ed., 1909, ii:139. Cited in *Oxford Dictionary of
Quotations*, 369.

40   **The realization of the deception...** *Die to Live*, 12.

41   **Things that matter most...** Widely attributed to Goethe
in online sites, but unable to confirm or find book reference.
Retrieved 3 December, 2003, from www.toinspire.com/author.
asp?author=Goethe.

42   **Put all your worries aside...** *Spiritual Letters*, 169:111.

42   **Nothing is true and nothing is false...** *Fabulas*, 25.

43   **To live in that atmosphere...** *Die to Live*, 206–207.

44   **Do your work, then withdraw...** See *Tao Te Ching*, IX:35.

44   **Lord Krishna advises his disciple...** *Bhagavad Gita*, III:7–11.

45   **Most high, almighty, good Lord...** *Francisco de Asis*, 224–225.

46   **Let Him accomplish things...** *The Science of the Soul,* 189:19.

46   **It is the business and duty...** *Spiritual Gems,* 321–322:200. Italics added by Esponda.

47   **The Master is waiting inside...** *Spiritual Gems,* 96:65. When, in the course of the disciple's inner evolution, the Radiant Form manifests itself within, it is the Master's feet that first appear at the eight-petalled lotus, a microcosmic centre on the astral plane. Hence the expression "feet" or "lotus feet" of the Master.

48   **Strive, struggle, grapple and wrestle...** Quoted in "It's the Effort That Makes the Difference", *Science of the Soul,* p. 27.

48   **taking tea at auntie's house...** *Kabir Sakhi Sangrah,* 43:1, translated in *Kabir: the Weaver of God's Name.*

49   **Sant Mat teaching is very simple...** *Die to Live,* 236:298.

50   **Our prayers and pleadings...** *The Science of the Soul,* 198:39.

50   **The first essential thing...** *Spiritual Gems,* 249:157. Italics in original book.

52   **If you take one step to take refuge...** *Kabitt Svaiyye,* 46.

53   **The aim should always be to increase...** *The Science of the Soul,* 159:70.

54   **Unless we discipline our mind...** *Die to Live,* 72:37.

54   **If we get time in the morning...** *Spiritual Discourses,* vol. 2, 220.

54   **Master Sawan Singh used to say...** Cited by Charan Singh in *Die to Live,* 256:332.

55   **If you force your mind to meditate...** *Die to Live,* 72:37.

56   **The journey of a thousand miles...** See *Tao Te Ching,* LXIV:137.

56   **I am well aware that you have struggles...** *Spiritual Gems,* 239:152.

57   **Do what you can as best you can...** *Light on Sant Mat,* 37.

58   **Our deepest fear is...** *A Return to Love: Reflections on the Principles of a Course in Miracles,* 219–220. Note that while this passage is widely attributed to Nelson Mandela's 1994 inaugural speech, our research indicates that it is from the above-referenced title and was not quoted in Mandela's inaugural speech.

59   **But Jesus beheld them...** Bible, *Matthew* 19:26.

60   **You just call out my name…** "You've got a Friend" from
         Tapestry (New York: Screen Gems, Columbia Music, Inc.,
         1971).

Chapter 3: Meditation is a way of life

61   **Meditation is a way of life…** *Die to Live*, 206.
63   **Life is what happens to you…** "Beautiful Boy (Darling
         Boy)" from *Lennon Legend: The Very Best of John Lennon*, (New
         York: Capitol Records, 1998).
63   **What will we wear…** See Bible, *Luke* 12:22–25.
64   **View'd from eternity, existence is …** *A Modern Imitation
         of Christ*, 183–184.
65   **There is something wrong with us…** *Die to Live*, 95–
         96:69.
65   **All work is his work…** *Spiritual Letters*, 132:84.
66   **No man is an island, entire of itself…** *John Donne, Dean
         of St. Paul's, Complete Poetry and Selected Prose*, 537–539.
67   **The worldly obligations you are fulfilling…** *Spiritual Letters*,
         95:59.
67   **Withdrawing our consciousness…** *Die to Live*, 93–94:68.
67   **Having once contacted it…** *Die to Live*, 16.
68   **Once the mind becomes fond of listening…** *Divine Light*,
         142.
69   **positive psychological and physiological effects…** For a
         review of research on this subject, see Murphy, M. and S. Dono-
         van, *The Physical and Psychological Effects of Meditation*.
70   **We should not be seeking…** *The Practice of the Presence of
         God*, 48:2.
70   **Meditation is nothing but a preparation…** *Die to Live*,
         137:137.
71   **I die daily…** Bible, *1 Corinthians* 15:31.
71   **What a blessing it would be…** Quoted in *Die to Live*, 25.
72   **Whatever the state of mind…** *Bhagavad Gita*, VIII:6.
73   **Die to live…** *Die to Live*, 135:133.
74   **Your breath is like a drumbeat…** *Sar Bachan Poetry*, 197.
         'Radha Soami' is the name with which Master Shiv Dayal Singh of
         Agra, known as Soami Ji Maharaj, designated the Supreme Being.

Chapter 4: The source of love and devotion

75   **Were it not for His grace...** *Die to Live,* 32.

75   **The Master not only guides...** *Die to Live,* 23.

76   **Our real Master is the Word...** *Die to Live,* 21.

76   **He that hath seen me...** Bible, *John* 14:9.

77   **Within me the Father has revealed...** Adi Granth, 1141.

77   **You can build love and devotion...** *Die to Live,* 63:29.

77   **The only way to strengthen love...** *Die to Live,* 63:29.

78   **The heart has its reasons...** *The Translations of Pensées,* tr.
          L. Brunschvicg, 5th ed., 1909, iv:277. Cited in *Oxford Dictionary
          of Quotations,* 369.

78   **Love came and emptied me of self...** *Nobody, Son of No-
          body,* 13:65.

79   **Emotions are all right if...** *Die to Live,* 107:87.

80   **When the celestial war drum...** *Kabir Sakhi Sangrah,* 20–
          21, translated in *Kabir, The Great Mystic.*

80   **The strongest warrior is...** Aztec saying.

81   **Love is always within...** *Die to Live,* 107:86.

82   **People think that by running...** *Spiritual Heritage,* 61–62.
          Disciples of Soami Ji of Agra and his successors often greet each
          other by saying "Radha Soami", the term used for the Supreme
          Being.

82   **Running after the physical form...** *Die to Live,* 107:86.

83   **Nevertheless I tell you...** Bible, *John* 16:7.

83   **Commenting on this quote...** *Light on Saint John,* 205.

85   **May your Love of the Form...** *Legacy of Love,* 547.

85   **The purpose of the physical form...** *Spiritual Heritage,* 156.

88   **A thousand miles away...** *Abyat-i-Bahu,* 169, translated in
          Sultan Bahu.

89   **Your desire to visit India...** *Spiritual Gems,* 203:141.
          Brahmand designates the entire created sphere, from the most sub-
          tle mental realms to the gross physical realms. Trikuti refers to the
          stage in the inner journey where the soul sheds its gross coverings.
          Sach Khand is the realm of pure spirit, the true home of the soul.

Chapter 5: The practice of meditation

91   **Be still, and know that I am God...** Bible, *Psalms* 46:10.

91   **Sitting quietly, doing nothing...** Zen saying.

98   **Meditation means trying to hold...** *Die to Live*, 44:7.
100   **Concentrate on keeping your mind...** *The Practice of the Presence of God*, 63–64.
101   **The third eye is the seat of the mind...** *Spiritual Discourses*, vol. 1. 180–181.
102   **When you close your eyes...** *Die to Live*, 115–116:98.
102   **Answering your question as to the best way...** *Spiritual Gems*, 241–243:154. Italics added by Esponda.
104   **Unless we withdraw our attention...** *Die to Live*, 16.
106   **The first step, then, is to withdraw...** *Die to Live*, 16.
106   **So long as we remain away from...** *Divine Light*, 63.
106   **Your wildest dreams or imaginings...** *Spiritual Gems*, 226–227:147.
107   **It is possible to pray at all times...** Quoted in *The Way of the Pilgrim and the Pilgrim Continues His Way*, 199.
108   **Please make no attempt...** *Spiritual Gems*, 309:198.
109   **There is no mode of life in the world...** *The Practice of the Presence of God*, 48:2.
110   **One who accustoms himself...** *The Way of the Pilgrim and the Pilgrim Continues His Way*, 9.
111   **No one can describe the glory...** *Sar Bachan Poetry*, 233.
111   **No one should give the answer...** Quoted in *The Way of the Pilgrim and the Pilgrim Continues His Way*, 199.
112   **Persons who repeat the holy names...** Quoted by Master Sawan Singh in *Philosophy of the Masters*, vol.1, 71. "Whenever the people sit they are surrounded by angels and covered by mercy, and there descends upon them tranquillity as they remember Allah." Hadith, *Sahih Muslim*, 35:6505.
113   **I keep myself in His presence...** *The Practice of the Presence of God*, 55:5.
113   **You do not need to speak out loud...** Qur'an, 20:7–8.
114   **Sugar, buffalo milk and chocolates ...** The actual quote is: "Sugar, molasses, honey and buffalo milk are all sweet, but they equal not the Lord." Adi Granth, 1379.
114   **O Beloved! I have heard many a tale ...** Quoted in *Philosophy of the Masters*, vol.1, 89.
116   **When your concentration...** *Spiritual Gems*, 308:198.
116   **On a dark night, Inflamed by love...** *San Juan de la Cruz*, 33–34.

117   **Bhajan simply means attending...** *Philosophy of the Masters,*
        vol.1, 94.

118   **Your attention may remain focused...** *Spiritual Letters,*
        112:70.

118   **When you sit in bhajan...** *Spiritual Letters,* 74–75:44.

120   **Devotion to the Shabd...** *Philosophy of the Masters,
        Abridged,* 214–215.

120   **The soul has penetrated...** *Shabdavali,* vol. 2, 11:28, trans-
        lated in *Tulsi Sahib, The Saint of Hathras.*

121   **You are not imagining things...** *Light on Sant Mat,*
        305:298.

Conclusion

123   **Brave is he who has control...** *Dawn of Light,* 162:60.

124   **I can tell you one thing: just attend...** *Die to Live,* 270–
        271:353.

For further reflection

127   **This world is perishable...** *Sar Bachan,* 3.

128   **To subjugate the mind...** *Spiritual Letters,* 73–74:44.

129   **An ounce of practice...** *The Science of the Soul,* 181.

130   **I am surprised at the people of this world...** *Sartha
        Tukaram Gatha,* 1496, translated in *Tukaram, The Ceaseless Song
        of Devotion.*

131   **In the beginning, we have to make...** *The Practice of the
        Presence of God,* 73.

132   **There's no set prayer...** *Die to Live,* 40:4.

133   **The light on your face...** *Nobody, Son of Nobody,* 15:81.

134   **The minute I heard...** *The Essential Rumi,* 106.

Books and Authors Cited

Abu-Saeed Abil-Kheir (967–1049)   A lawyer-theologian who was highly honoured by followers of Islam, Abu-Saeed was known as the "Socrates of the Sufi Path". This Sufi mystic often referred to himself as "nobody, son of nobody"—his expression of the reality that his life was surrendered in the divine. From Khurasan, an area that is now part of Iran and Afghanistan, Abu-Saeed preceded the great poet Jalaluddin Rumi by over two hundred years on the same path of annihilation in love.

Adi Granth   Known also as *Sri Guru Granth Sahib*, the Adi Granth is comprised primarily of writings of the Gurus in the line of Guru Nanak, but it also includes verses from many other saints from the Indian subcontinent. It was compiled and edited by the fifth guru, Guru Arjun Dev, at the end of the sixteenth century.

Bahu, Sultan (1629?–1691)   Hazrat Sultan Bahu, a disciple of Sayyid Abdur Rahman Qadiri, was one of the great Sufi saints of the Indian subcontinent. He was not formally educated, but is said to have written more than a hundred works in Persian and Arabic. However, it is his poems in the Punjabi language that live on and remain popular among the people of Punjab.

143

Bhagavad Gita   Literally '*Song of the Lord*', the *Bhagavad Gita* embodies the teachings of Lord Krishna given in the dialogue between Krishna and his disciple Arjuna on the battlefield of the Mahabharata war. It is one of the most popular books of Hindu philosophy.

Bible   The term Bible, or *Holy Bible*, refers to the sacred scriptures of Judaism and Christianity. The Jewish Bible, written mostly in Hebrew, is divided into the Torah (Five Books of Moses), Prophets, and Writings. It recounts the history of mankind from the time of the Creation, the lives of the Patriarchs and early Israelites, and the teachings of their prophets and holy men. The Christian Bible is made up of the Old Testament, which includes the books of the Jewish Bible, and the New Testament, which consists of writings pertaining to the life and teachings of Jesus Christ and his disciples. It contains the four Gospels, the Epistles (letters from some of the disciples), the Acts of the Apostles, and Revelations (also known as the Apocalypse).

Blake, William (1757–1827)   English poet, painter, and engraver, Blake created a unique form of illustrated verse. His poetry, inspired by mystical vision, is among the most original, lyric, and prophetic in the English language. Blake's most famous works of art are the twenty-one illustrations in *Inventions to the Book of Job*.

Bulleh Shah (1680–1758)   Born into a high-class Muslim family, Saa'in Bulleh Shah grew up in Kasur, near Lahore. He incurred the wrath of his community when he became a disciple of the mystic saint Inayat Shah of Lahore, a simple gardener. His poetry and songs of mystical love and longing are still recited and sung in India and Pakistan.

Campoamor, Ramon de (1817–1901)   The first Spanish poet to break with the romantic tradition of long, tragic, and emotional poetry, de Campoamor's humorous short poems are collected in *Dolores, Pequeños Poemas,* and *Humoradas.* At one time he was the governor of Castellon and made primary education mandatory in his province.

Charan Singh (1916–1990)   Born in Moga, Punjab, India, Maharaj Charan Singh was a disciple of Maharaj Sawan Singh of Radha Soami Satsang Beas. Maharaj Ji, as he was widely called, was a lawyer by profession. In 1951 Maharaj Jagat Singh made him his successor, and for the next four decades Maharaj Ji travelled throughout India and the world, giving discourses and initiating seekers. Teaching about the Word, he often stressed looking beyond differences of race, culture and religion. His teachings have been recorded in several books containing his writings, talks and letters. Before his death in 1990, he appointed Baba Gurinder Singh as his successor.

Chrysostom, John (c. 349–407)   Born in Antioch in Syria (now Antakya, Turkey), Saint John Chrysostom studied oratory under the Greek rhetorician Libanius, later became an ordained priest and eventually became known for the eloquence, earnestness and practical nature of his preaching, such that he gained a reputation as the greatest orator of the early church. John Chrysostom's many works include homilies, epistles, treatises and liturgies.

Cloud of Unknowing   A devotional classic of the Protestant tradition, *Cloud of Unknowing* sprang from an age when English mysticism was in full flower. The author is unknown, but is thought to be an English priest who lived during the latter half of the fourteenth century.

Dhammapada *(Path of Truth)*   The author of the verses in the *Dhammapada* is unknown, although they are believed to be the teachings of the Buddha himself. The text of the book was established by the time of the great Buddhist Emperor, Ashoka, in the third century B.C.

Donne, John (1572–1631)   A London-born English poet, prose writer and clergyman, John Donne is considered the greatest of the metaphysical poets and one of the most profound writers of love poetry. His *Devotions upon Emergent Occasions* focuses on the themes of death and human relationships.

Epictetus (c. 55–135)   Regarded as a Greek Stoicist, Epictetus was born in Hierapolis in Phrygia (modern-day Turkey). As a boy he landed in Rome as a slave and studied with the Stoic teacher Musonius Rufus. After being freed, he went to Greece where he opened his own school. It appears that Epictetus wrote nothing himself. The works that present his philosophy were written by his student, Flavius Arrian.

Farid (c. 1181–1265)   Sheikh Farid, or Baba Farid, a Muslim saint whose verses are preserved in the Adi Granth, was the earliest-known mystic poet in Punjabi. Born near Multan (now in Pakistan), Farid undertook rigorous self-discipline and physically punishing methods in his attempt to achieve his goal of God-realization. Eventually, he was advised to go to Khwaja Qutubuddin Bakhtiar Kaki of Delhi, who revealed to him the path of the Word.

Francis of Assisi (c. 1182–1226)   Born in Assisi, Saint Francis was an Italian mystic and preacher who was famous for his ability to communicate with all living creatures. He also performed charities among the lepers and worked at restoring dilapidated churches. Saint Francis founded the Franciscan order of monks and was canonized in 1228. In 1980 Pope John Paul II proclaimed him patron saint of ecologists.

Goethe, Johann Wolfgang (1749–1832)   Goethe was a German poet, dramatist, novelist and scientist. At first involved in a movement advocating romantic and emotional artistry, he later adopted a more classic writing style. *Faust*, the first great work of literature in the spirit of modern individualism, was the ultimate achievement of Goethe's long life. In this allegory of human life, Goethe emphasized the right of the individual to enquire freely into affairs both human and divine and to work out his own destiny.

Gurdas, Bhai (c. 1558–1637)   Bhai Gurdas Ji was a mystical poet who was a contemporary of the fourth, fifth and sixth Gurus in the line of Guru Nanak. He is traditionally believed to have been the scribe who, under the supervision of Guru Arjun, collected together the writings that became the Adi Granth. He wrote the *Kabitt Svaiyye* and the *Varan*.

Guru Amar Das (1479–1574)   The third successor in the line of Guru Nanak, Guru Amar Das, from Punjab, came to his master, Guru Angad, late in life at the age of sixty-one. He is credited with starting the institution of the langar (free community kitchen). His extensive writings are included in the Adi Granth.

Guru Arjun (1563–1606)   Guru Arjun was the fifth Guru in the line of Guru Nanak. Through great effort, Guru Arjun Dev collected, classified and compiled the writings of the Adi Granth, including compositions of saints from all over the Indian sub-continent whose teachings emphasize the oneness of God, the path of the Word, the equality of all people and the pursuit of truth.

Guru Nanak (1469–1539)   Born at Talwandi near Lahore in present-day Pakistan, Guru Nanak Dev spent a large part of his life travelling to spread the teachings of the Word or Divine Name. He was the first in the line of the ten Gurus whose teachings are recorded in the Adi Granth, which has become the sacred scripture of the Sikhs. He endeavoured to transform the prejudices and superstitions of the people, emphasizing that ritualistic practices and external forms of worship kept the seeker of God away from the truth.

Hafiz (c. 1326–1390)   Khwaja Hafiz, one of the greatest Persian poets, was born Shams-al-Din Muhammad in Shiraz. His *Diwan-i-Hafiz*, a compendium of *ghazals* or love poems, is universally acknowledged not only as a work of great literary merit but also as one with considerable mystic import. His poetry is well known today in both the East and the West.

Humilis, Clemens (c. 1900s)   Not much can be ascertained about the life of Clemens Humilis, but it is known that he was a parish priest who published *Vox Domini* in 1929 and *Vox Dilecti* in 1931. *A Modern Imitation of Christ*, a book of spiritual advice written in poetic form and published in London, is a compendium of the two earlier works.

Jagat Singh (1884–1951)   Born in the village of Nussi not far from Beas, Punjab, India, Maharaj Jagat Singh was initiated when he was twenty-six years old by Maharaj Sawan Singh.

Following his retirement in 1943 as vice-principal of the Punjab Agricultural College, he spent the remainder of his life in his Master's service at Beas. In 1948 Sardar Bahadur Jagat Singh was appointed by his Master to be his successor. *The Science of the Soul*, a compilation of his discourses and excerpts from his letters to seekers and disciples, was published after his death.

Jaimal Singh (1839–1903)   Born into an agricultural family in Ghuman, Punjab, India, Baba Jaimal Singh, widely known as Baba Ji Maharaj, was initiated by Soami Ji Maharaj of Agra and directed by him to propagate the Sant Mat teachings in Punjab. After retiring from military service, he chose a secluded place on the west bank of the Beas River to pursue uninterrupted meditation. Soon seekers started visiting him, laying the foundation for organized satsang at Beas. Several months before his death in 1903, he appointed Maharaj Sawan Singh as his successor. It was the latter who named the place Dera Baba Jaimal Singh in honour of his master's memory. Baba Ji Maharaj's letters to Maharaj Sawan Singh have been published in the form of a book entitled *Spiritual Letters*.

John of the Cross (1542–1591)   Saint John of the Cross was a Spanish mystic and poet. Born in Fontiveros, Spain, he became a Carmelite monk in 1563 and was ordained as a priest in 1567. His attempts at monastic reform led to his imprisonment, and it was there that he began to compose some of his finest work, including the poems *Cántico espiritual* (Spiritual Canticle) and *Llama de amor viva* (Living Flame of Love). In his best-known lyric, *Noche obscura del alma* (Dark Night of the Soul), Saint John described the soul's progress in seeking and finally attaining union with God through an experience parallel to Christ's crucifixion and glory.

Kabir (c. 1398–1518)   Born in Kashi (Banaras or Varanasi), Kabir Sahib eked out a meagre living weaving cloth. Teaching the practice of the Word, he travelled throughout India and attracted a large following of disciples, Hindus as well as Muslims. Kabir faced unrelenting opposition from the priestly class for his outspoken condemnation of rituals and the outward show of religion. Today, his verses are popular throughout India and the versatility and power of his poetry are widely acknowledged.

King, Carole (1949–)   Born Carole Klein in Brooklyn, New York, Carole King is a popular American singer and songwriter who recorded the album *Tapestry* in the 1970s. In the early 1980s King moved to rural Idaho and became an environmental activist.

Lawrence, Brother (1611–1691)   Born Nicholas Herman in Lorraine, France, Brother Lawrence of the Resurrection lived most of his life in a Carmelite monastery where he suffered from a feeling of anxiety that he was clumsy and stupid and didn't do anything right. He decided that he would just hand over his worries to the Lord by talking to him as his close friend. Some of his letters and conversations were compiled into a short book entitled *The Practice of the Presence of God.*

Lennon, John Winston (1940–1980)   This British songwriter and singer composed some of the most popular songs of his era. Born in Liverpool, Lennon was the co-writer, along with Paul McCartney, of most of the songs that distinguished the phenomenal career of the Beatles through the 1960s. He was assassinated outside his home in New York.

Muhammad (570?–632)   The Prophet Muhammad was born in Mecca and lived in what is now Saudi Arabia. Called 'the

Messenger', he brought the Muslim teachings to the people of his time and taught the importance of worshipping the one God, Allah. The message revealed to him is recorded in the Qur'an, and traditions concerning his life and teachings are found in the Hadith.

Pascal, Blaise (1623–1662)   A French philosopher, mathematician and physicist, Pascal was one of the eminent scientists of his day and also a great mystical writer. He espoused Jansenism, a Christian reform movement that advocated strict morality and austerity, and in 1654 entered the Jansenist community at Port Royal, where he led a rigorously ascetic life until his death eight years later.

Patanjali (200 B.C.?)   Patanjali was the compiler and editor of the *Yoga Sutras*, the earliest systematic treatise on yoga. He described an eight-step system designed to free the body and mind from restlessness and impurity and to control, unify and direct bodily and psychic energy towards higher consciousness and liberation.

Qur'an   The Qur'an is the sacred scriptures of Islam, written in Arabic and said to be revealed to the Prophet Muhammad in the beginning of the 7th century. It consists of 114 chapters covering many different topics—sacred, legal, social and scientific.

Rumi (1207–1273)   Jalaluddin Rumi, known respectfully in India as Maulana Rum (the learned man of Rum), was of Persian origin from Balkh. He moved to Konya, Turkey, where he became a religious teacher. There he met Shams-i-Tabrez and became his disciple. Rumi wrote the *Masnavi* and *Diwan-i Shams-i Tabrez*, both of which have contributed to his contemporary status as one of the most well-known Sufi mystics and poets, popular in both the East and the West.

Sardar Bahadur   *See* Jagat Singh

Sasaki, Sokei-an (1882–1945)   Son of a Japanese Shinto priest, Sokei-an Sasaki arrived in San Francisco in 1906 with the mission of bringing Zen to America. He wrote his autobiography, *Holding the Lotus to the Rock*, as America's first Zen Buddhism master.

Sawan Singh (1858–1948)   Maharaj Sawan Singh, affectionately called the Great Master, was born in the village Jatana near Mehmansinghwala, District Ludhiana, Punjab, India. He was initiated by Baba Jaimal Singh, who appointed him as his successor in 1903. Thereafter, for forty-five years he assiduously served as the Master at the Radha Soami Satsang Beas, spreading the teachings of Sant Mat in India and abroad. His books include the *Gurmat Siddhant (Philosophy of the Masters)*, an encyclopaedia of the teachings of the saints, as well as two volumes of letters written to Western disciples and a volume of his discourses.

Shaw, George Bernard (1856–1950)   Irish-born writer and Nobel laureate, Shaw is considered one of the most significant British dramatists since Shakespeare. Shaw moved to London in 1876, and by the mid-1880s, he became, and remained, a firm believer in vegetarianism and never drank spirits, coffee or tea. Shaw's major play, *Heartbreak House*, exposed the spiritual bankruptcy of his generation, and he received the Nobel Prize for *Saint Joan*. His comic masterpiece, *Pygmalion*, was the basis for the musical comedy and film *My Fair Lady*.

Shiv Dayal Singh   *See* Soami Ji

Soami Ji (1818–1878)   Born Shiv Dayal Singh in Agra, India, Soami Ji was raised on the scriptures of the Adi Granth. He started preaching the way of the Word after spending the greater part of seventeen years meditating. Through his two books *Sar Bachan* (prose) and *Sar Bachan Poetry*, he gave out the universal teachings of the saints in unveiled, simple Hindi.

Tao Te Ching   It is difficult to know much for certain about the origins of the *Tao Te Ching (The Book of the Way and Its Power)*, a fundamental Taoist text that espouses the way of the Tao, the timeless ultimate principle, which is followed through simplicity, humility, and non-binding action. The *Tao Te Ching* was probably compiled before the latter half of the third century B.C., but it is thought that the book is based on Chinese oral tradition that may even antedate the written word. The author of the *Tao Te Ching* is commonly referred to as Lao-Tzu or Lao Tse (there are many variants in English), but modern scholars doubt that he actually existed. It is probable that 'Lao-Tzu', which means both 'the old philosopher' and 'the old philosophy', refers to the ancient origin of the varied material within the text.

Tukaram (1598–1650)   Reared in a well-to-do family of traders in the Indian state of Maharashtra, Tukaram was blessed with initiation by Babaji Raghavachaitanya in 1619. He composed thousands of poems in Marathi, the local language, denouncing all outward forms of worship and urging people to devote themselves to the Name. His poems, which remain popular today, are published under the titles *Sartha Tukaram Gatha* and *Shri Tukaram Maharaj Yanchya Abhanganchi Chhandabaddha Gatha*.

Tulsi Sahib (1763–1848)   The great poet-saint of Hathras and author of the *Ghat Ramayana,* Tulsi Sahib was born in the princely family of the Peshwas. He began to show signs of a devotional trend of mind at an early age and had no desire for worldly pleasures and pursuits. He settled in Hathras near Agra, Uttar Pradesh, India, where he was known as Dakkhini Baba. Soami Ji's mother was a disciple of Tulsi Sahib long before Soami Ji was born, and Soami Ji had contact with him from his childhood.

The Way of a Pilgrim and the Pilgrim Continues His Way   A classic nineteenth-century Russian text by an unknown author, this is an account of an anonymous wanderer who set out on a journey across Russia with nothing but a backpack, some bread and a Bible—and a burning desire to learn the true meaning of the words of Saint Paul, "pray without ceasing," and to put them into action.

Williamson, Marianne (1952–)   An American author and lecturer in the fields of spirituality and new age thought, she wrote the best sellers *A Return to Love* and *Everyday Grace,* among other books. She teaches the basic principles of "A Course in Miracles" and discusses their application to daily living.

Bibliography

Abu-Saeed Abil-Kheir. *Nobody, Son of Nobody.* Translated by Vraje Abramian. Prescott, Arizona: Azholm Press, 2001.

Adi Granth. *Shabdarath Sri Guru Granth Sahib Ji.* 4 vols. Amritsar: Shromani Gurdwara Prabandhak Committee, 1999.

Bahu, Sultan. *Abyat-i-Bahu.* Edited by Sultan Altaf Ali. Lahore: Alfaruq Book Foundation, 1975.

———. In *Sultan Bahu.* J.R. Puri and K.S. Khak. (1st ed. 1998) 2nd ed. Beas, Punjab: Radha Soami Satsang Beas, 1999.

Bible. *The Holy Bible.* London: Oxford University Press, n.d. *(Authorized Version).*

Bulleh Shah. In *Bulleh Shah.* J.R. Puri & T.R. Shangari. (1st ed. 1986) 2nd ed. Beas, Punjab: Radha Soami Satsang Beas, 1995.

———. *Kulliyat Bulleh Shah.* Edited by Faqir Mohammad Faqir. Lahore: Punjabi Adabi Academy, 1970.

Campoamor, Ramon de. *Fabulas.* Oviedo, Spain: Editorial Biblioteca Filosofia en Espanol, 2003.

Charan Singh. *Die to Live.* (1st ed. 1979) 7th ed. Beas, Punjab: Radha Soami Satsang Beas, 1999.

155

————. *Divine Light.* (1st ed. 1967) 7th ed. Beas, Punjab: Radha Soami Satsang Beas, 1996.

————. *Light on Saint John.* (1st ed. 1967) 6th ed. Beas, Punjab: Radha Soami Satsang Beas, 1994.

————. *Light on Sant Mat.* (1st ed. 1958) 9th ed. Beas, Punjab: Radha Soami Satsang Beas, 1997.

————. *Quest for Light.* (1st ed. 1972) 6th ed. Beas, Punjab: Radha Soami Satsang Beas, 2002.

————. *Spiritual Discourses.* Vol. 1. English translation. (1st ed. 1964) 7th ed. Beas, Punjab: Radha Soami Satsang Beas, 1996.

————. *Spiritual Discourses.* Vol. 2. English translation. Beas, Punjab: Radha Soami Satsang Beas, 1997.

————. *Spiritual Heritage.* (1st ed. 1983) 3rd ed. Beas, Punjab: Radha Soami Satsang Beas, 1998.

The Dhammapada. Translated by S. Radhakrishnan. London: Oxford University Press, 1950.

Donne, John. *John Donne, Dean of St. Paul's: Complete Poetry and Selected Prose.* Edited by John Hayward. London: The Nonesuch Press, 1941.

Epictetus. *Epictetus: The Art of Living: A New Interpretation by Sharon Lebell.* Translated by Sharon Lebell. New York: Harper Collins Publishers Inc, 1995.

Francis of Assisi. In *Francisco de Asis.* Juan Bautista Montorsi. 23rd ed. Mexico City: Ediciones Paulinas, S.A. de C.V., 2001.

Gurdas, Bhai. *Kabitt Svaiyye.* Amritsar: Shromani Gurdawara Parbandhak Committee, 1956.

Hafiz. *I Heard God Laughing: Renderings of Hafiz.* Translated by Daniel Ladinsky. Walnut Creek, California: Sufism Reoriented, 1996.

Humilis, Clemens. *A Modern Imitation of Christ.* London: A.R. Mowbray & Co. Limited, 1960.

Jagat Singh. *The Science of the Soul.* (1st ed. 1959) 10th ed. Beas, Punjab: Radha Soami Satsang Beas, 1996.

Jaimal Singh. *Spiritual Letters.* English translation. (1st ed. 1958) 7th ed. Beas, Punjab: Radha Soami Satsang Beas, 1998.

John of the Cross. In *San Juan de la Cruz.* Elizabeth Matthew. Mexico City: Editorial Verdad y Vida, S.A. de C.V., n.d.

Kabir. *Kabir Sakhi Sangrah.* Reprint, Allahabad: Belvedere Printing Works, 1996.

————. In *Kabir, The Great Mystic.* Isaac A. Ezekiel. (1st ed. 1966) 6th ed. Beas, Punjab: Radha Soami Satsang Beas, 2003.

————. In *Kabir, The Weaver of God's Name.* V. K. Sethi. (1st ed. 1984) 3rd ed. Beas, Punjab: Radha Soami Satsang Beas, 1998.

Lao Tzu. *Tao Te Ching.* Translated by J. Duyvendak. London: John Murray Ltd, 1954.

Lawrence, Brother. *The Practice of the Presence of God.* Translated by John J. Delaney. New York: Doubleday, 1977.

Legacy of Love. Beas, Punjab: Radha Soami Satsang Beas, 2000.

Murphy, M. and S. Donovan. *The Physical and Psychological Effects of Meditation.* Sausalito, CA: Institute of Noetic Science, 1999.

Oxford Dictionary of Quotations. 3rd ed. Oxford: Oxford University Press, 1979.

Patanjali. *How to Know God: Yoga Aphorisms of Patanjali.* Translated by Swami Prabhavanada and Christopher Isherwood. London: George Allen & Unwin Ltd., 1953.

Rumi, Jalaluddin. *Discourses of Rumi*. Translated by A. J. Arberry. London: John Murray Ltd, 1961.

———. *The Essential Rumi*. Translated by Coleman Barks. San Francisco: HarperSanFrancisco, 1995.

Sasaki, Sokei-an. *The Little Zen Companion*. Translated by David Schiller. New York: Workman Publishing, 1994.

Sawan Singh. *Dawn of Light*. (1st ed. 1985) 2nd ed. Beas, Punjab: Radha Soami Satsang Beas, 1989.

———. *Discourses on Sant Mat*. English translation. (1st ed. 1963) 5th ed. Beas, Punjab: Radha Soami Satsang Beas, 1993.

———. *Philosophy of the Masters*. Vol.1. English translation. (1st ed. 1963) 6th ed. (Revised). Beas, Punjab: Radha Soami Satsang Beas, 1996.

———. *Philosophy of the Masters*. Vol. 4. English translation. (1st ed. 1967) 5th ed. Beas, Punjab: Radha Soami Satsang Beas, 1997.

———. *Philosophy of the Masters*. Abridged. English translation. (1st ed. 1973) 5th ed. Beas, Punjab: Radha Soami Satsang Beas, 1997.

———. *Spiritual Gems*. (1st ed. 1958) 9th ed. (Revised). Beas, Punjab: Radha Soami Satsang Beas, 1996.

Schotel, Barbara. "It's the Effort That Makes the Difference". *Science of the Soul* 34:1 (March, 1996).

Soami Ji [Shiv Dayal Singh]. *Sar Bachan*. English translation. (2nd ed. 1955) 10th ed. Beas, Punjab: Radha Soami Satsang Beas, 1999.

———. *Sar Bachan Poetry (Selections)*. English translation. 1st ed. Beas, Punjab: Radha Soami Satsang Beas, 2002.

Tukaram. *Sartha Tukaram Gatha*. 3 vols. P. N. Joshi. Mumbai: Shri Bharat Book Depot, 1968.

————. In *Tukaram, The Ceaseless Song of Devotion.* Chandravati Rajwade. (1st ed. 1978) 3rd ed. Beas, Punjab: Radha Soami Satsang Beas, 2004.

Tulsi Sahib. *Shabdavali.* Vol. 2. Allahabad: Bellevedere Press, 1972.

————. In *Tulsi Sahib, Saint of Hathras.* J.R. Puri and V.K. Sethi. (1st ed. 1978) 3rd ed. Beas, Punjab: Radha Soami Satsang Beas, 1995.

The Way of a Pilgrim and the Pilgrim Continues His Way. Translated by R.M. French. 2nd ed. London: The Society of Promoting Christian Knowledge, 1954.

Williamson, Marianne. *A Return to Love: Reflections on the Principles of a Course in Miracles.* New York: Harper Collins, 1992.

Addresses for Information and Books

INDIAN SUB-CONTINENT

INDIA
The Secretary
Radha Soami Satsang Beas
P.O. Dera Baba Jaimal Singh 143204
District Amritsar, Punjab

NEPAL
Mr. Dal Bahadur Shreshta
Radha Soami Satsang Beas
P. O. Box 1646, Gongabu, Dhapasi,
Kathmandu

PAKISTAN
Dr. Bhagwandas M. Pathai
Resham Gali, Larkana, Sindh

SRI LANKA
Mr. D. H. Jiwat
c/o Geekay Ltd.
33 Bankshall Street, Colombo 11

SOUTHEAST ASIA

*Representative for other countries
of Far-East Asia:*

Mrs. Cami Moss
Radha Soami Satsang Beas, Hostel 6
P.O. Dera Baba Jaimal Singh 143204
District Amritsar, Punjab, India

MALAYSIA
Mr. Selvarajoo Pragasam
No. 15 Jalan SL 10/4,
Bandar Sg. Long,
43000 Kajang

THAILAND
Mr. Harmahinder Singh Sethi
58/32 Rachdapitsek Road, Soi 16
Thapra, Bangkok Yai 10600

INDONESIA
Mr. Ramesh Sadarangani
Jalan Pasir Putih IV/16, Block E 4 Ancol
Timur, Jakarta Utara 14430

PHILIPPINES
Mr. Kay Sham
Radha Soami Satsang Beas
#1268 General Luna Street
Paco, Manila

SINGAPORE
Mrs. Asha Melwani
Radha Soami Satsang Beas
19 Amber Road, Singapore 439868

ASIA PACIFIC

AUSTRALIA
Mr. Pradeep Raniga
P.O. Box 642
Balwyn North, Victoria 3104

161

NEW ZEALAND
Mr. Tony Waddicor
Science of the Soul Study Centre
P. O. Box 5331
Auckland

GUAM
Mrs. Hoori M. Sadhwani
115 Alupang Cove
241 Condo Lane, Tamuning 96911

HONG KONG
Mr. Manoj Sabnani
T.S.T., P.O. Box 90745
Kowloon

JAPAN
Mr. Jani G. Mohinani
Radha Soami Satsang Beas
1-2-18 Nakajimadori
Aotani, Chuo-Ku
Kobe 651-0052

SOUTH KOREA
Dr. Moon Jin Hee
#2011 Jung San 4RI Buron-Myun
Won Ju-City
Kang Won Do
Korea 220-814

TAIWAN, R.O.C.
Mr. Larry Teckchand Nanwani
P. O. Box 68-1414
Taipei

NORTH AMERICA

CANADA
Mr. John Abel
#701-1012 Beach Avenue
Vancouver, B.C. V6E 1T7

Mrs. Meena Khanna
149 Elton Park Road
Oakville, Ontario L6J 4C2

UNITED STATES
Dr. Vincent P. Savarese
3507 Saint Elizabeth Road
Glendale, CA 91206-1227

Science of the Soul Study Center
2415 East Washington Street
Petaluma, CA 94954

Dr. Frank E. Vogel
71 Old Farm Road
Concord, MA 01742

Science of the Soul Study Center
4115 Gillespie Street
Fayetteville, NC 28306-9053

Dr. John Templer
114 Verdier Road
Beaufort, SC 29902-5440

Mr. Hank Muller
1900 North Loop West, Suite 500
Houston, TX 77018

CARIBBEAN

Representative for the Caribbean, Suriname and Guyana:

Mr. Sean Finnigan
P. O. Box 2314
Port-au-Prince
Haiti, W. I.

BARBADOS
Mr. Deepak Nebhani
Radha Soami Satsang Beas
Lot No. 10, 5th Avenue
Belleville, St. Michael
Barbados, W. I.

CURACAO
Mrs. Komal Lachman Vasandani
P. O. Box 426
Curacao, N. A.

GUYANA
Mrs. Rajni B. Manglani
A-80 Eping Avenue,
Bel Air Park,
Georgetown, Guyana

JAMAICA
Mrs. Shammi Khiani
P. O. Box 22
Montego Bay
Jamaica, W. I.

ST. MAARTEN
Mrs. Kanchan Mahbubani
R.S.S.B. Foundation
P. O. Box 978
Phillipsburg
St. Maarten, N. A.

SURINAME
Mr. Chandru Samtani
15 Venus Straat
Paramaribo
Suriname

TRINIDAD
Mrs. Anganie Chatlani
8A Saddle Road, Maraval
Trinidad, W. I.

CENTRAL AMERICA

BELIZE
Mrs. Chand Babani
5789 Goldson Avenue, Belize City

MEXICO
Mr. Jorge Angel Santana
Jacarandas #30
FTO. Azaleas Recidencial
Zapopan 45090

PANAMA
Mr. Deepak Dhanani
Altos Del Bosque
Residencial El Doral, Casa 195
Republica De Panama

SOUTH AMERICA

*Representative for other countries of
South America (Argentina, Brazil,
Chile):*

Mr. Hiro W. Balani
P.O. Box 486,
Malaga 29012, Spain

COLOMBIA
Mrs. Emma Orozco
P. O. Box 49744, Medellin

ECUADOR
Dr. Fernando Flores Villalva
Calle de la Grulla, lote 11
Urbanizacion Valle 3 - Cumbaya
Quito

PERU
Mrs. Haseen Mirpuri
Av. Benavides 120-901, Peru
Miraflores, Lima

VENEZUELA
Radha Soami Satsang Beas
Avenida Las Samanes
c/c Calle Los Naranjos
Conjunto Florida 335, Urb. La Florida
Caracas

EUROPE

AUSTRIA
Mr. Hansjorg Hammerer
Sezenweingasse 10, Salzburg A-5020

BELGIUM
Mr. Piet J. E. Vosters
Lindekensstraat 39 Box 4
Turnhout 2300

BULGARIA
Mr. Emilio Saev
Foundation Radha Soami Satsang Beas
Bulgaria
P. O. Box 39, 8000 Bourgas

CYPRUS
Mr. Heraclis Achilleos
P. O. Box 29077, Nicosia 1035

CZECH REPUBLIC
Mr. Vladimir Skalsky
Maratkova 916,
142 00 Prague 412

DENMARK
Mr. Tony Sharma
Sven Dalsgaardsvej 33
DK-7430 Ikast

FINLAND
Ms. Ritta Anneli Wingfield
Hansinkatu 12 C 33
01400 Vantaa near Helsinki

FRANCE
Ct. Pierre de Proyart
7 Quai Voltaire, Paris 75007

GERMANY
Mr. Rudolf Walberg
P. O. Box 1544
D-65800 Bad Soden / Taunus

GIBRALTAR
Mr. Sunder Mahtani
Radha Soami Satsang Beas
Flat 401 Ocean Heights, 4th Floor
Queensway

GREECE
Mrs. Eleftheria Tsolaki
P.O. Box 35
Paleo Faliro 17503, Athens

ITALY
Mrs. Wilma Salvatori Torri
Via Bacchiglione 3, 00199 Rome

*THE NETHERLANDS
(HOLLAND)*
Radha Soami Satsang Beas - Nederland
Middenweg 145 E
1394 AH Nederhorst den Berg

NORWAY
Mr. Sohan Singh Mercy
St. Halvardsgt. 6
N-3015 Drammen

POLAND
Mr. Vinod Sharma
UL. 1go Sierpien 36 B M-100
PL-02-134, Warsaw

PORTUGAL.
Mrs. Sharda Lodhia
Rua Quinta Das Palmeiras, Lote 68
11° andar C, Oeiras 2780-145

ROMANIA
Mrs. Carmen Cismas
C.P. 6-12
Braila-810474

SLOVENIA
Mr. Marko Bedina
Brezje pri Trzicu 68
4290 Trzic

SPAIN
Mr. J. W. Balani
Calle Panorama no. 15
Cerrado de Calderon
Malaga 29018

SWEDEN
Mr. Lennart Zachen
Norra Sonnarpsvägen 29
S-286 72 Asljunga

SWITZERLAND
Mr. Sebastian Zust-Bischof
Weissenrainstrasse 48
CH 8707 Uetikon am See (ZH)

UNITED KINGDOM
Mr. Narinder Singh Johal
Haynes Park Estate
Haynes, Bedford MK45 3BL

AFRICA

BENIN
Mr. Jaikumar T. Vaswani
01 Boite Postale 951,
Recette Principale, Cotonou

BOTSWANA
Dr. Krishan Lal Bhateja
P. O. Box 402539, Gaborone

GHANA
Mr. Murli Chatani
Radha Soami Satsang Beas
P. O. Box 3976, Accra

IVORY COAST
Mr. Konan N'Dri
08 Boite Postale 569
Abidjan 08

KENYA
Mr. Surinder Singh Ghir
P. O. Box 15134,
Langata 00509, Nairobi

LESOTHO
Mr. Sello Wilson Moseme
P. O. Box 750
Leribe 300

LIBYA (G.S.P.L.A.J.)
Mr. Roshan Lal
P.O. Box 38930
Bani Walid

MAURITIUS
Mrs. Doolaree Nuckcheddy
17 Avenue Le Conte De Lisle
Quatre Bornes

NAMIBIA
Mrs. Jennifer Mary Carvill
P. O. Box 1258
Swakopmund 9000

NIGERIA
Mr. Nanik N. Balani
P.O. Box 10407, Lagos

RÉUNION
Ms. Danielle Hoareau
23 Rue Juiliette Dodu
97400 St. Denis

SIERRA LEONE
Mr. Kishore S. Mahboobani
P. O. Box 369
Freetown

SOUTH AFRICA
Radha Soami Satsang Beas
14-16 Hope Street
Gardens Cape Town
Waterfront 8002

Mr. Gordon Clive Wilson
P. O. Box 47182, Greyville 4023

Mr. Sam Busa
P. O. Box 41355, Craighall 2024

SWAZILAND
Mr. Peter Dunseith
P. O. Box 423, Mbabane

TANZANIA
Mr. Surinder Singh Oshan
P.O. Box 6984, Dar-Es-Salaam

UGANDA
Mr. Sylvester Kakooza
Radha Soami Satsang Beas
P. O. Box 31381, Kampala

ZAMBIA
Mr. Chrispin Lwali
P. O. Box 12094
Nchanga, North Township
Chingola, Lusaka

ZIMBABWE
Mrs. Dorothy Roodt
P. O. Box 7095, Harare

MIDDLE EAST

BAHRAIN
Mr. Mangat Rai Rudra
Flat No. 12 Building No. 1694
Road No. 627, Block 306
Manama

ISRAEL
Mr. Michael Yaniv
Moshav Sde Nitzan
D.N. Hanegev 85470

KUWAIT
Mr. Vijay Kumar
P. O. Box 1913
13020 Safat

U.A.E.
Mr. Mohanlal Badlani
R.S.S.B.
P.O. Box 37816
Dubai

Books on This Science

SOAMI JI MAHARAJ
Sar Bachan Prose
Sar Bachan Poetry (Selections)

BABA JAIMAL SINGH
Spiritual Letters (to Hazur Maharaj Sawan Singh: 1896-1903)

MAHARAJ SAWAN SINGH
The Dawn of Light (letters to Western disciples: 1911-1934)
Discourses on Sant Mat
My Submission (introduction to *Philosophy of the Masters*)
Philosophy of the Masters (*Gurmat Sidhant*), in 5 volumes
    (an encyclopedia on the teachings of the Saints)
Spiritual Gems (letters to Western disciples: 1919-1948)
Tales of the Mystic East (as narrated in satsangs)

MAHARAJ JAGAT SINGH
The Science of the Soul (discourses and letters: 1948-1951)

MAHARAJ CHARAN SINGH
Die to Live (answers to questions on meditation)
Divine Light (discourses and letters: 1959-1964)
Light on Saint John
Light on Saint Matthew
Light on Sant Mat (discourses and letters: 1952-1958)
The Master Answers (to audiences in America: 1964)
The Path (first part of *Divine Light*)
Quest for Light (letters: 1965-1971)
Spiritual Discourses, in 2 volumes
Spiritual Heritage (from tape-recorded talks)
Thus Saith the Master (to audiences in America: 1970)

BOOKS ABOUT THE MASTERS
Call of the Great Master—Diwan Daryai Lal Kapur
Heaven on Earth—Diwan Daryai Lal Kapur
Treasure Beyond Measure—Shanti Sethi
With a Great Master in India—Julian P. Johnson
With the Three Masters, in 2 volumes—from the diary of
    Rai Sahib Munshi Ram

INTRODUCTION TO SPIRITUALITY
A Spiritual Primer—Hector Esponda Dubin
Honest Living: A Means to an End—M. F. Singh
The Inner Voice—Colonel C. W. Sanders
Liberation of the Soul—J. Stanley White
Life is Fair: The Law of Cause and Effect—Brian Hines

BOOKS ON MYSTICISM
A Treasury of Mystic Terms, Part I: The Principles of Mysticism
    (6 volumes)—John Davidson
The Holy Name: Mysticism in Judaism—Miriam Caravella
Yoga and the Bible—Joseph Leeming

BOOKS ON SANT MAT IN GENERAL
In Search of the Way—Flora E. Wood
Living Meditation: A Journey beyond Body and Mind
   —Hector Esponda Dubin
Message Divine—Shanti Sethi
The Mystic Philosophy of Sant Mat—Peter Fripp
Mysticism, The Spiritual Path, in 2 volumes—Lekh Raj Puri
The Path of the Masters—Julian P. Johnson
Radha Soami Teachings—Lekh Raj Puri
A Soul's Safari—Netta Pfeifer

MYSTICS OF THE EAST SERIES
Bulleh Shah—J. R. Puri and T.R. Shangari
Dadu, The Compassionate Mystic—K. N. Upadhyaya
Dariya Sahib, Saint of Bihar—K. N. Upadhyaya
Guru Nanak, His Mystic Teachings—J. R. Puri
Guru Ravidas, Life and Teachings—K. N. Upadhyaya
Kabir, The Great Mystic—Isaac A. Ezekiel
Kabir, The Weaver of God's Name—V. K. Sethi
Mira, The Divine Lover—V. K. Sethi
Saint Namdev—J. R. Puri and V. K. Sethi
Saint Paltu—Isaac A. Ezekiel
Sarmad, Jewish Saint of India—Isaac A. Ezekiel
Sultan Bahu—J. R. Puri and K. S. Khak
Tukaram, The Ceaseless Song of Devotion—C. Rajwade
Tulsi Sahib, Saint of Hathras—J. R. Puri and V. K. Sethi